MORE
TRUE
FACTS
THAT
SOUND
LIKE
Bull$#*t

13-Digit ISBN: 978-1-60433-995-6
10-Digit ISBN: 1-60433-995-0

This book may be ordered by mail from the publisher.
Please include $5.99 for postage and handling. Please support your local bookseller first!
Books published by Cider Mill Press Book Publishers are available at special discounts for
bulk purchases in the United States by corporations, institutions, and other organizations.
For more information, please contact the publisher.

Cider Mill Press Book Publishers
"Where good books are ready for press"
PO Box 454
12 Spring Street
Kennebunkport, Maine 04046
Visit us online!
cidermillpress.com

Typography: Adobe Caslon Pro, Festivo Letters No1,
Capriccio, Microbrew One, Trade Gothic LT Std
Illustrations by Rebecca Pry

Printed in the USA
3 4 5 6 7 8 9 0

MORE TRUE FACTS THAT SOUND LIKE Bull$#*t

500 MORE INSANE-BUT-TRUE FACTS
TO RATTLE YOUR BRAIN

CIDER MILL PRESS

BOOK PUBLISHERS
KENNEBUNKPORT, MAINE

[CONTENTS]

{ Introduction }

We all love a good story, and the stranger or more unlikely, the better! The world and the universe beyond it have no shortage of unlikely facts that don't sound real, and they are all the more satisfying when they turn out to be true. This little book offers you a compilation of the curious and examples of the extraordinary. In it, you'll find facts about history, music, science, entertainment, food, and more that on first reading, you'd think couldn't possibly be true. But truth is indeed stranger than fiction. Okay, maybe not all the time, but often enough that it can (and should) make us question our assumptions about the world we live in.

Collections of facts and stories are kind of a thing nowadays. The internet is awash in "fact" sites that repeat the same stories over and over, but often some of those "facts" are untrue, or misinterpreted. It's easy enough to copy and paste material from one site to another, but sometimes investigating behind the scenes reveals that the "fact" is actually an urban legend, or even just a meme going around because it sounds good and drives traffic. A warning: some of these fake facts have made it into this book in the form of True or False questions, so have fun and be careful about getting tripped up

It's always fun to learn more about the amazing world around us, so have fun flipping through these pages, and enjoy your excursion into the amazing world of true facts that sound like bullsh*t!

History

HISTORY IS FULL OF WEIRD FACTS

History is far more than just names and dates. It's all about real people who lived real lives. But it's even more than that: it's about real people who lived really strange lives. Or witnessed very odd events. Or found themselves in the middle of totally unexpected circumstances.

Whether it's in regard to a single life or an entire nation, history always has interesting things to tell us, from the earliest of times to just yesterday. There's an old Chinese curse that says: "May you live in interesting times," and as these facts show, some of those times were very interesting, indeed.

1. THERE REALLY WAS A DRACULA.

He lived from 1431 to 1476 and was prince of a small country called Wallachia, in what is now southern Romania. He was famed for resisting Ottoman Turkish invasions and for his incredible cruelty. He executed tens of thousands of people, most horribly by impaling many on wooden stakes, earning him the nickname "Vlad the Impaler." There's no evidence that he drank blood, though.

2. KING HENRY VI OF ENGLAND (1421-1471) WAS VERY RELIGIOUS.

Once, at a Christmas feast, he was said to have fled from it in terror because a group of dancers showed up to perform in the nude.

3. LATE NINETEENTH-CENTURY DOCTORS WARNED WOMEN ABOUT A NEW DISEASE CALLED BICYCLE FACE.

This was described as the danger of getting stuck with the expressions they made while on their bikes, such as flushed face, bulging eyes, clenched jaw, and other such things, all due to the exertion it took to ride. Some warned it might be permanent, while others said it would go away over time, if bike riding were abandoned. No, it wasn't a real thing.

· 4 ·

ONCE WHILE HUNTING, NAPOLEON WAS ATTACKED BY A SWARM OF HUNDREDS (OR MAYBE EVEN THOUSANDS) OF RABBITS AND HAD TO FLEE IN HIS COACH.

The bunnies weren't wild, they were released for the hunt and thought that Napoleon and his entourage were bringing them food.

5. GEORGE WASHINGTON OPENED A WHISKEY DISTILLERY.

This was after he had served as president of the United States, of course.

6. VICTORIAN DOCTORS BELIEVED THAT MEN WHO GREW BEARDS COULD WARD OFF ILLNESS.

Beards were seen as air filters that could prevent "impurities" from entering the body.

7. IN DETROIT IN THE 1930s, STREET SWEEPER JOSEPH FIGLOCK WAS HIT BY TWO FALLING BABIES.

The first hit him when he was cleaning an alley and the baby fell from a window; both survived. A year later, Figlock was cleaning another alley, and another baby fell from a window above and also struck him. Again, both survived.

8. DURING THE MIDDLE AGES AND RENAISSANCE, GROUPS OF PEOPLE SOMETIMES DANCED THEMSELVES TO DEATH.

This bizarre affliction, Choreomania (also called the "dancing plague"), was well documented. One person would start dancing in public, and gradually others would join in over the next few days, as if it were contagious. Some wouldn't or couldn't stop, and would die. These plagues could go on for days or weeks.

9. **ROMANS BELIEVED THAT DRINKING THE BLOOD OF SLAIN GLADIATORS COULD CURE EPILEPSY.**

No word on whether or not it worked.

10. **JOHN TYLER (1790-1862), THE TENTH PRESIDENT OF THE UNITED STATES, HAS TWO GRANDSONS WHO ARE STILL ALIVE AS OF 2019.**

Tyler fathered children late in life, one of whom also fathered children late in life.

11. **ROBERT G. HEFT WAS A 17-YEAR-OLD STUDENT WHEN HE DESIGNED THE CURRENT U.S. FLAG.**

It was a school assignment, and he received a *B-* grade. His teacher told him his grade would improve if the U.S. adopted his design as the official flag. It did and he was given an A.

• 12 •

PRESIDENT ANDREW JACKSON'S PET PARROT HAD TO BE REMOVED FROM HIS FUNERAL IN 1845 BECAUSE IT WOULDN'T STOP SWEARING.

Well, someone must have taught it all those words!

13. ENGLISH THEOLOGIAN JOHN WILKINS (1614–1672) SUGGESTED THAT FLYING CHARIOTS COULD TAKE HUMANS TO THE MOON.

He believed that other people lived there who could and would become trade partners with England.

14. CUBAN LEADER FIDEL CASTRO SURVIVED OVER 600 ASSASSINATION ATTEMPTS.

This is according to Cuba's former counterintelligence chief; the CIA alone explored unorthodox options, from exploiting Castro's love of scuba diving (by trying to lure him to pick up a bomb-wired seashell) to his habit of smoking cigars (by spiking a box of his favorites with a botulinum toxin).

15. IN THE LATE 1920s, THERE WAS A PROPOSED BAN AGAINST WOMEN SMOKING.

Women organized and marched against the proposal and retained their right to light up.

16. FORKS WERE ONCE SEEN AS SACRILEGIOUS.

In the eleventh century, a young Greek woman, a niece of the Byzantine emperor, married a powerful Venetian. At the feast, she used a gold fork, which was condemned as an affront to God. When she died young, many saw it as proof of her sin of vanity.

17. A WOMAN WAS ELECTED TO THE HOUSE OF REPRESENTATIVES BEFORE AMERICAN WOMEN WERE ALLOWED TO VOTE.

Jeanette Rankin became the first woman in Congress in 1916, four years before women gained the right to vote.

18. PHARAOH PEPI II NEFERKARE (TWENTY-THIRD CENTURY BCE) HATED FLIES.

He ordered his servants and slaves to be smeared with honey to attract them and keep himself free of them. We don't know what the servants thought about this.

19. "SAY PRUNES!"

Great Britain's first portrait photographer, Richard Beard, was said to have asked his subjects to say "prunes" instead of "cheese" to get the desired mouth shape. A big smile was not in fashion then, apparently.

20. THERE WAS A SECRET BAVARIAN CATHOLIC SOCIETY KNOWN AS THE ORDER OF THE PUG (FOUNDED CA. 1740).

The order required its novices to wear dog collars and scratch at the door to be let in, and they were led around blindfolded while members barked at them; the society was banned in 1748.

• 21 •

DURING THE LATER MIDDLE AGES, ANIMALS WERE SOMETIMES PUT ON TRIAL FOR CRIMES.

They could be sentenced if found guilty, including to death.

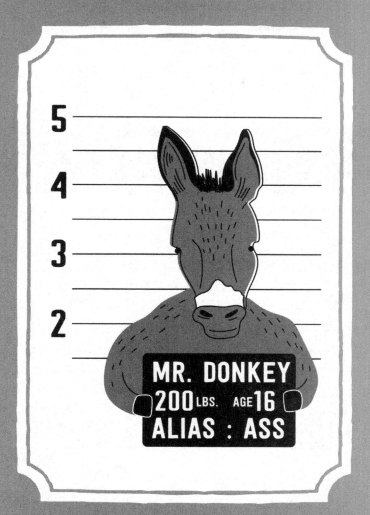

22. THE WORLD'S OLDEST CONTINUALLY-FUNCTIONING PARLIAMENT IS OVER 1,000 YEARS OLD.

The Althing of Iceland was founded in 930 CE, Some claim that the Tynwald of the Isle of Man is also over 1,000 years old, though there is less evidence to prove it. Both were founded by Vikings.

23. JOSEPH STALIN WAS TWICE NOMINATED FOR THE NOBEL PEACE PRIZE, IN 1945 AND 1948.

To be fair, a nomination doesn't mean the committee will take the candidate seriously. Hitler was nominated, too.

24. IN 1918, DURING WORLD WAR I, SOME U.S. RESTAURANTS RENAMED THEIR HAMBURGERS AS "LIBERTY STEAKS" TO AVOID THE GERMAN-SOUNDING NAME.

This was another example of the "freedom fries" mentality that emerged surrounding the Iraq War, only over eighty years earlier.

25. IT WAS ONCE THOUGHT THAT THE SOVIET UNION TEMPORARILY RAN OUT OF VODKA.

With the announcement that Nazi Germany had surrendered on May 9, 1945, there was so much celebrating in Russian cities that supplies were cleaned out.

26. SADDAM HUSSEIN WAS GIVEN THE KEY TO THE CITY OF DETROIT IN 1980.

The mayor, Coleman A. Young, gave out more than 100 keys during his time in office, including this one, in recognition of Hussein's $500,000 donation to a local Iraqi church in need of repair.

27. DANISH EXPLORER PETER FREUCHEN (1886-1957) SAVED HIMSELF FROM BEING BURIED ALIVE IN AN AVALANCHE WITH A POOP DAGGER.

Trapped under the avalanche in Greenland without his usual tools, Freuchen fashioned a dagger made of his own frozen feces and dug his way out.

28. WE LIVE CLOSER TO THE HEIGHT OF THE ROMAN EMPIRE THAN THE ROMANS LIVING THEN DID TO THE BUILDING OF THE PYRAMIDS OF GIZA IN EGYPT.

The Pyramids were constructed from about 2550 to 2490 BCE, and the height of the Roman Empire was in the first century. So we're closer by about 400 years!

29. THOMAS JEFFERSON AND JOHN ADAMS DIED ONLY A FEW HOURS APART AND ON THE SAME DAY, JULY 4, 1826.

This date was also the fiftieth anniversary of the signing of the Declaration of Independence. Adams's last words were, "Thomas Jefferson survives." But, in fact, Jefferson had died about five hours earlier.

• 30 •

IN EIGHTEENTH-CENTURY ENGLAND, THE WEALTHY AND FASHIONABLE COULD RENT A PINEAPPLE (EXPENSIVE AND RARE AT THE TIME) FOR A DAY OR AN EVENING.

It wasn't eaten, but was carried around to impress their friends at social functions.

31. PHOTOGRAPHING ONE'S DEAD RELATIVES WAS POPULAR IN VICTORIAN ENGLAND.

Given high mortality rates, some families would arrange solo shots or family portraits that included a child (or even an adult) who had just died. This might be the only photograph they would have of the relative in question, so it became a treasured possession.

32. WOMEN IN RENAISSANCE (AND LATER) FRANCE COULD TAKE THEIR HUSBANDS TO COURT FOR BEING IMPOTENT.

Said husband would then have to prove that it wasn't true. Imagine what an ordeal that was.

33. FRANK HAYES (1888-1923) WAS DEAD WHEN HE WON A HORSE RACE AT BELMONT PARK, NEW YORK.

Despite suffering a heart attack halfway through the race, Hayes's body stayed on the horse, Sweet Kiss, and he was first across the finish line.

34. ONE OF THE MOST SUCCESSFUL PIRATES OF ALL TIME WAS A CHINESE WOMAN WHO LIVED DURING THE LATE EIGHTEENTH AND EARLY NINETEENTH CENTURIES.

Ching Shih (1775–1844) terrorized China, commanding over 300 junks (ships) and by some estimates, up to 50,000 pirates.

35. THE SHORTEST WAR IN HISTORY LASTED FOR 38 MINUTES.

In Zanzibar in 1896, Sultan Hamad bin Thuwaini died, or was possibly murdered by his cousin Khalid, who assumed the throne. The British were not happy about this, and after a brief assault on the palace, Khalid fled. The Anglo-Zanzibar War of 1896 was over just as it started.

36. IN 1998, CONSERVATIONISTS DOING REPAIRS ON BENJAMIN FRANKLIN'S OLD LONDON HOME DISCOVERED 1,200 PIECES OF BONE BELONGING TO AT LEAST FIFTEEN HUMAN BODIES.

He was no secret mass murderer, however. The bodies were used for anatomical study in a medical school on the site, run by Franklin's friend.

37. THE "D" IN "D-DAY" SIMPLY STANDS FOR "DAY."

Use of "D" is a military designation to mark the start of an operation. "D+1" would stand for one day after D-Day. They also use "H-Hour" in the same way.

38. THE SHORTEST TERM IN OFFICE OF ANY U.S. PRESIDENT WAS ONE MONTH.

President William Henry Harrison took the oath of office on March 4, 1841, and died on April 4, 1841.

• 39 •

SINCE 1945, ALL BRITISH ARMORED VEHICLES (TANKS AND SO ON) HAVE INCLUDED EQUIPMENT FOR MAKING TEA.

Cheerio!

· 40 ·

LORD BYRON KEPT A PET BEAR AT THE UNIVERSITY OF CAMBRIDGE.

He was told that dogs were not permitted, so he brought a bear instead, pointing out that the university rules didn't forbid them. He was allowed to keep the animal and took it for walks around the city. He also tried to get it enrolled as a student. In this, at least, he failed.

41. A LARGE NUMBER OF MEDIEVAL SCHOLARS DIDN'T WRITE THEIR OWN BOOKS.

Well, they "wrote" them in the sense that they were the authors, but quite a few dictated their words to scribes, who actually wrote those words down.

42. MEDIEVAL ENGLAND WAS PRETTY EMPTY OF PEOPLE.

Compared to its current population of about fifty-six million, for much of the Middle Ages, the English population wasn't much more than three million. And with the Black Death (plague) sweeping through in the fourteenth century, that number shrunk even more.

43. ABOUT ONE IN EIGHT WOMEN IN RENAISSANCE FLORENCE (SIXTEENTH CENTURY) WAS A NUN.

Guaranteed food and shelter, plus a community of like-minded individuals, nunneries offered safety and security in a society where women often had few protections.

44. LASAGNA WAS A POPULAR MEDIEVAL FOOD AMONG THE UPPER CLASSES.

Known in English cookbooks as "losyns," it was sheets of thin pasta layered with cheese. Of course, they didn't yet have tomatoes, but they were well on their way.

45. SHOES WITH HEELS WERE FIRST WORN BY MEN.

Persian soldiers in the tenth century discovered that having a heel helped keep their feet in their horses' stirrups. In seventeenth century Europe, heeled shoes became a fashion item, but were still mainly worn by rich men.

46. PEOPLE IN EUROPE IN THE SIXTEENTH AND SEVENTEENTH CENTURIES MOSTLY DRANK BEER WHEN THEY WERE THIRSTY.

Water supplies were unreliable and could be unsafe, unless boiled. So low-alcohol beer was the perfect solution.

47. PRESIDENT LYNDON B. JOHNSON USED TO GIVE INTERVIEWS FROM THE BATHROOM.

He didn't want to have to stop a conversation.

48. WINSTON CHURCHILL WAS KNOWN TO SMOKE UP TO TEN CIGARS A DAY.

Still, he lived to be ninety years old.

49. THE IRON MAIDEN NEVER EXISTED.

The first mentions of this medieval torture and execution device didn't appear until the eighteenth century, and it seems to be a fiction made up to make earlier times seem more gruesome than they already were.

· 50 ·

GIRAFFES WOULD SOMETIMES WANDER THROUGH THE STREETS OF RENAISSANCE FLORENCE.

They were kept by wealthy families, such as the Medici, and once in a while they got loose from their pens. That must have been a sight!

51. IN 1672, A DUTCH LEADER AND STATESMAN NAMED JOHAN DE WITT WAS EATEN BY AN ANGRY MOB.

He had neglected the Dutch army, which suffered a number of defeats, and was already unpopular. He also attempted to help his brother, who was about to be exiled, when a group attacked them both in a planned assassination attempt. After that, things got out of hand, they were strung up, and their livers cooked and eaten.

52. IN THE LATER EIGHTEENTH CENTURY, SOME WEALTHY ENGLISH WOULD HIRE "HERMITS" TO LIVE ON THEIR ESTATES.

These old men would live in a "hut" or hermitage and be trotted out as a curiosity to guests. Assuming their needs were taken care of, it might not have been a bad way to spend one's last years.

53. BRIDGET DRISCOLL WAS KILLED IN LONDON IN 1896, AFTER BEING HIT BY A CAR THAT WAS TRAVELING AT ABOUT FOUR MILES PER HOUR.

One witness said the car was speeding at a dangerous pace, "like a fire engine."

54. INTO THE NINETEENTH CENTURY, PEOPLE SLEPT TWICE DURING THE NIGHT.

They'd go to sleep for three to four hours, usually at sunset, wake up for a couple hours to do things, and then go back to sleep until sunrise.

55. KING FAROUK I OF EGYPT (1920-1965) WAS A KLEPTOMANIAC.

Though he was rich beyond belief, he had a compulsion to steal things. He once stole Winston Churchill's pocket watch (later claiming to have "found" it, when a search was conducted), but he also simply took what he wanted from Egypt's elite, from paintings to pianos, since as king, no one could refuse him.

56. HUNDREDS OF THOUSANDS OF CHILDREN SERVED IN THE AMERICAN CIVIL WAR.

Many were in non-combat roles, such as musicians, but it's been estimated that 100,000 Union soldiers were fifteen years old or younger.

57. CARS WERE NOT INVENTED IN THE UNITED STATES.

The first automobile was invented by Karl Benz and Emile Levassor in Germany.

58. HEROIN WAS ONCE PRESCRIBED AS A MEDICINE.

It was a popular late nineteenth-century cure-all, given for everything from headaches to coughs to insomnia.

· 59 ·

NUNS STARTED BITING EACH OTHER IN FIFTEENTH-CENTURY GERMANY FOR NO GOOD REASON.

The biting started at a convent in Germany, but spread as far as Italy and the Netherlands. Demonic possession was thought of as a possible cause, but mass hysteria seems likely. The "biting fever" eventually died down, but it's never been fully explained.

• 60 •

JULIUS CAESAR WAS ONCE KIDNAPPED BY PIRATES IN THE AEGEAN SEA.

The pirates demanded a ransom of twenty pieces of silver (more than $500,000) for his release. He laughed at the price, saying that he was worth no less than fifty!

61. TRUE OR FALSE? PEOPLE SUSPECTED OF BEING WITCHES WERE HEAVILY PERSECUTED DURING THE MIDDLE AGES.

False. In general, the church taught that magic and witchcraft were superstitious nonsense, and trials and persecutions of accused witches were rare before the sixteenth century.

62. TRUE OR FALSE? IN EARLY TWENTIETH-CENTURY AMERICA, STAGED TRAIN CRASHES WERE POPULAR.

True. A good steam train crash show was like the demolition derby of its time. They were put on a single track and set to run into each other.

63. TRUE OR FALSE? KETCHUP WAS ORIGINALLY A DESSERT.

False. It was originally sold as a remedy for indigestion.

64. TRUE OR FALSE? THE VICTORIANS ATE FLAMING FRUIT.

True. In a game called "Snapdragon," the rules called for players to put raisins in a bowl, cover them with rum, and set them on fire. The objective was to fish out a raisin and eat it while it was still burning!

65. TRUE OR FALSE? BENJAMIN FRANKLIN WANTED THE TURKEY TO BE THE NATIONAL BIRD OF THE UNITED STATES, RATHER THAN THE BALD EAGLE.

False. It's a popular story, and Franklin did indeed write that he preferred the turkey, but it was meant as a joke. Franklin was fond of satire, but sometimes others didn't get it.

66. TRUE OR FALSE? THE PILGRIMS REALLY DID WEAR BUCKLES ON THEIR HATS.

False. That image comes from much later, in the nineteenth century.

67. TRUE OR FALSE? PRESIDENT ZACHARY TAYLOR DIED AFTER EATING TOO MANY OYSTERS.

False. It was actually after eating too many cherries, resulting in acute gastroenteritis. The food may have been contaminated, but for a while rumors circulated that he had been poisoned.

68. TRUE OR FALSE? IN 1912, A PARIS ORPHANAGE HELD A RAFFLE TO RAISE MONEY, AND THE PRIZES WERE LIVE BABIES.

True. It was well intentioned, with the goal of finding homes for children with suitable parents.

• 69 •

TRUE OR FALSE?
THE ROMANS HAD A GODDESS
OF THE SEWERS.

True. Her name was Cloacina and she
presided over keeping the water system of
Rome clean, a noble goal.

70. TRUE OR FALSE? A WAR BETWEEN THE NETHERLANDS AND THE ISLES OF SCILLY LASTED FOR 335 YEARS.

True. Known as the 335 Year War (naturally!), it lasted from 1651 to 1986. The Dutch decided to back Cromwell in the English Civil War, and the Royalists considered this a betrayal. With the Royalist navy harboring at the Isles of Scilly off the coast of Cornwall, the Dutch navy demanded reparations for Royalist attacks. The Royalists refused and the Dutch declared war. No shots were ever fired, but no peace treaty was ever signed, until it was finally completed in April 1986.

71. TRUE OR FALSE? PEOPLE IN THE MIDDLE AGES ONLY USUALLY LIVED TO BE THIRTY YEARS OLD.

False. The average age of medieval Europeans is skewed by the high infant mortality rate, but if someone made it to twenty-one, they stood a good chance of living past fifty, and even to their mid-sixties.

72. TRUE OR FALSE? VICTORIANS HAD "SAFETY COFFINS" TO PREVENT THEM FROM BEING BURIED ALIVE.

True. Apparently, it happened often enough that a mechanism for ringing a bell was installed, letting those trapped underground call for help, should they wake up in a tight spot.

73. TRUE OR FALSE? COWBOYS IN THE "OLD WEST" DIDN'T WEAR COWBOY HATS.

True. They preferred bowler hats, actually.

74. TRUE OR FALSE? PYTHAGORAS FORBADE HIS FOLLOWERS FROM EATING BEANS.

True. We're really not sure why.

75. TRUE OR FALSE? PAUL REVERE FAMOUSLY SHOUTED "THE BRITISH ARE COMING!"

False. He had to make the ride in secret; shouting anything would have been very foolish. Also, the colonists still considered themselves to be British at the time, so shouting that would have made no sense.

76. TRUE OR FALSE? IN LONDON'S FIRE OF 1666, ONLY SIX PEOPLE DIED.

False. That number has been recorded, and another says that only eight people died, but realistically, the numbers of unreported and undocumented dead must have been much higher.

77. TRUE OR FALSE? IN THE BRITISH HOUSE OF COMMONS, THE SPEAKER OF THE HOUSE IS NOT ALLOWED TO SPEAK.

True. The role of the Speaker is to moderate debate and ensure that the rules are followed.

• 78 •

TRUE OR FALSE? DANISH ASTRONOMER TYCHO BRAHE (EARLY SEVENTEENTH CENTURY) HAD A PET MOOSE THAT LIKED TO DRINK BEER.

True. He also lost his nose in a duel and had to wear a fake metal one for the rest of his life.

• 79 •

TRUE OR FALSE? MARIE-ANTOINETTE FAMOUSLY SAID "LET THEM EAT CAKE," ABOUT HER STARVING SUBJECTS.

False. It's unlikely she ever said this, since the same story (or similar versions) was also attributed to various other members of the French royal family, going back to the seventeenth century. She just became the focus of this callous attitude during the French Revolution.

80. TRUE OR FALSE? WALT DISNEY WAS CRYOGENICALLY FROZEN AFTER HIS DEATH.

False. He was cremated.

81. TRUE OR FALSE? ANCIENT EGYPTIANS HAD PILLOWS MADE OF STONE.

True. But these were used for the dead. They were ornately carved and meant as a fitting resting place for the head for all of eternity.

82. TRUE OR FALSE? WILMER MCLEAN (1814-1882) LIVED AT THE EXACT PLACES WHERE THE CIVIL WAR STARTED AND ENDED.

True. He owned a home near Manassas, Virginia, at the site of the Battle of Bull Run (1861), and then moved to Appomattox, Virginia, to get away from the conflict. But Robert E. Lee later surrendered to Ulysses S. Grant in 1865 at this very house. So much for escaping the war!

83. TRUE OR FALSE? THERE WAS ONCE A MUSTACHE STRIKE IN FRANCE.

True. French upper-class men wanted to forbid those in the "serving classes" from sporting facial hair, desiring to keep it for themselves. As a result, waiters went on strike in 1907 for higher wages and the right to wear a mustache. It only took two weeks for them to win their new rights and keep their facial hair!

84. TRUE OR FALSE? PRESIDENT RICHARD NIXON WAS A GIFTED MUSICIAN WHO PLAYED FIVE DIFFERENT INSTRUMENTS.

True. He played piano, violin, saxophone, clarinet, and accordion.

· 85 ·

TRUE OR FALSE? BEFORE TREES WERE BIG, THE EARTH WAS COVERED WITH GIANT MUSHROOMS.

True. Between 420 and 350 million years ago, organisms that were probably fungi stood as tall as twenty-four feet high and three feet wide and dominated the primeval landscape. You could top a lot of pizzas with one of those!

Music

MAD MUSIC FACTS, THEN AND NOW

Music may be the food of love, and it may soothe the savage breast (not beast, as it is often misquoted), but it can also be home to a lot of very strange stories. From Gregorian chant to rock 'n' roll, there is no shortage of odd facts and trivia about all things musical.

These tidbits are a small sampling of some of the more unusual things to be found in all genres of music. Classical, jazz, pop, and more offer up an abundance of strangeness to delight our reading eyes as much as the music itself pleases our listening ears.

1. FREDERICK CHOPIN FEARED BEING BURIED ALIVE.

The composer arranged for his heart to be removed after his death. It rests in Warsaw, while his body lies in Paris.

2. CARLO GESUALDO, A FAMOUS AND ECCENTRIC RENAISSANCE COMPOSER, WAS A MURDERER.

He was both a count and a prince, and was known to be troubled. When he discovered his wife's affair with another man in 1594, he killed them both with a sword. But since he was a member of the nobility, he couldn't be prosecuted under the law, so he got away with it. That doesn't seem very fair!

3. SEVENTEENTH-CENTURY COMPOSER JEAN BAPTISTE LULLY ACCIDENTALLY KILLED HIMSELF WITH A STAFF.

In the days before conductors used batons, they would sometimes have a staff that they tapped on the floor to keep the orchestra together and in time. Lully once accidentally hit his toe with just such a staff. He didn't attend to it, and it became infected. The infection spread and eventually killed him.

· 4 ·

THE DEVIL INSPIRED EIGHTEENTH-CENTURY COMPOSER GIUSEPPE TARTINI'S GREATEST WORK.

He once dreamed that he handed the Devil his violin to see what he could do with it, and the Prince of Darkness played the most amazing piece Tartini had ever heard. When he woke up, he tried to recreate it, but he said the final product couldn't compare with the one in his dream. He called it "The Devil's Trill."

5. BACH AND HANDEL BOTH LOST THEIR SIGHT IN LATER LIFE, AFTER BOTCHED OPERATIONS BY THE SAME QUACK DOCTOR.

Both composers had failing eyesight and both turned to the same man, a fake doctor named John Taylor, who had been getting away with fraud for a long time. Taylor went blind before he died too. Maybe a bit of poetic justice?

6. COMPOSER FRANZ JOSEPH HAYDN'S HEAD WAS LOST AFTER HIS DEATH.

When Haydn died in 1809, an admirer named Joseph Rosenbaum wanted to use it for phrenology, a fake science popular at the time, which held that examining the skull could give clues about an individual's personality. He arranged to steal it, and no one noticed until 1820. The skull was passed around to different owners and only reunited with its body in 1954.

7. FRENCH COMPOSER ERIC SATIE CLAIMED THAT HE ONLY ATE WHITE-COLORED FOODS.

A noted eccentric, he was fond of jokes and satire, but he once wrote that he would only eat foods like eggs, sugar, salt, rice, coconut, and certain kinds of fish (white ones, probably). He may have been lying.

8. TWENTIETH-CENTURY COMPOSER ARNOLD SCHOENBERG HAD A TERRIBLE FEAR OF THE NUMBER THIRTEEN.

Born on September 13 and died on July 13, he avoided the number when at all possible, even refusing to go into buildings with "13" in their address, as well as thirteenth floors. He also died at the age of seventy-six, and of course, 7+6=13.

9. NO ONE NOTICED WHEN RUSSIAN COMPOSER SERGEI PROKOFIEV DIED.

That's because he died on the same day as Stalin. Even the leading music journal devoted 115 pages to Stalin's death; Prokofiev got a mention on 116, the last page.

10. IN SARASOTA, FLORIDA, IT'S ILLEGAL TO SING IN PUBLIC WHILE ONLY WEARING A BATHING SUIT.

This is a holdover law from "simpler" times when showing too much skin was scandalous.

11. A GROUP OF PEOPLE KNOWN AS THE FLAGELLANTS WANDERED EUROPE SINGING PENITENTIAL SONGS AND WHIPPING THEMSELVES DURING THE BLACK DEATH OF THE 1350s.

They believed the plague was a punishment from God, and by whipping themselves they could atone for their sins. The sight of large numbers of people, all bloody from self-whipping, singing as they marched through towns and villages must have been eerie.

· 12 ·

MEDIEVAL AND RENAISSANCE BARBERSHOPS WERE ALSO PLACES FOR MAKING MUSIC AND BEING BLED.

Back in the day, barbers were known as barber-surgeons, and they not only cut hair, they would bleed people (a small amount of regular bleeding was considered good for one's health). In Tudor times, these shops also had musical instruments on hand, so customers could make music while waiting for their appointments.

13. NINETEENTH-CENTURY COMPOSER ANTON BRUCKNER ONCE CRADLED BEETHOVEN'S SKULL.

Bruckner practically worshipped Beethoven, so when his grave was opened to move his remains in 1888, Bruckner had to see them. He pushed his way to the front, reached down, and cradled the skull in his arms before being pulled away.

14. THE LITTLE TUNE "THREE BLIND MICE" MIGHT BE BASED ON THE EXECUTIONS OF ENGLISH PROTESTANTS BY QUEEN MARY IN THE MID-SIXTEENTH CENTURY.

She is known to have ordered the executions of over 300 people in the 1550s, and the rhyme might refer to their torture and death. "Cut off their tails with a carving knife" indeed!

15. A LARGE NUMBER OF MUSICIANS HAVE DIED AT THE AGE OF TWENTY-SEVEN.

Sometimes called the "27 Club," the supposed curse has hit many promising musicians (as well as actors, artists, and others) in the twentieth century, including: Brian Jones (Rolling Stones), Janis Joplin, Jim Morrison (The Doors), Jimi Hendrix, Ron "Pigpen" McKernan (Grateful Dead), Kurt Cobain (Nirvana), and Amy Winehouse.

16. TCHAIKOVSKY HATED HIS FAMOUS "1812 OVERTURE."

It was filled with Russian nationalism and sentiment, and he later remarked that it was "very loud and noisy and completely without artistic merit."

17. A MINI ICE AGE MAY HAVE CONTRIBUTED TO THE WORLD'S GREATEST VIOLINS.

Stradivarius violins are considered to be among the finest ever made. When Antonio Stradivari was building them in the seventeenth century, Europe was in the grips of a centuries-old cold weather pattern, which affected how trees grew and the thickness of their wood. This unique blend of weather and materials may well have contributed to how the wood conducted sound, meaning that these instruments will never be repeated exactly.

18. COMPOSER GUSTAV HOLST'S "THE PLANETS" IS BASED ON ASTROLOGY, NOT ASTRONOMY.

Holst was an amateur astrologer who cast horoscopes for friends. While his most famous work, "The Planets," seems like an astronomical tribute, it was actually based on each planet's astrological traits.

19. BEETHOVEN DEDICATED HIS THIRD SYMPHONY TO NAPOLEON, AND THEN REVOKED IT.

The Eroica, or "Heroic" Symphony was dedicated to Napoleon, but Beethoven changed his mind out of fear of losing money from a noble patron. But when Napoleon later declared himself emperor, Beethoven was enraged and pulled off the score's title page, tearing it in two and tossing it out a window. He condemned Napoleon for his ego and presumption.

• 20 •

CLASSICAL MUSIC MAKES PLANTS GROW FASTER.

On the other hand, heavy metal band Motörhead once joked that if they moved in next door to you, your lawn would die.

21. LISTENING TO A SONG MAKES YOU LIKE IT MORE, NOT LESS.

Contrary to the idea that hearing a song over and over makes you sick of it, research shows that you're more likely to enjoy it if you hear it often. This might explain why the same songs get played constantly on radio and streaming sites.

22. TCHAIKOVSKY'S PATHÉTIQUE SYMPHONY MAY HAVE BEEN CURSED. IN THE 1950s, THE NOTTINGHAM ORCHESTRA CANCELLED ALL PERFORMANCES OF THE SYMPHONY, BECAUSE EACH TIME IT WAS PERFORMED, AN ORCHESTRA MEMBER DIED.

An orchestra in Stockholm defied the ill omen and performed it. Sure enough, a clarinet player named Ludwig Warschewski collapsed and died on stage during the performance!

23. CELEBRATED PIANIST ANDRÉ TCHAIKOWSKY (NO RELATION TO THE COMPOSER) LEFT HIS SKULL TO THE ROYAL SHAKESPEARE COMPANY WHEN HE DIED IN 1982, SO HE COULD "PORTRAY" YORICK IN HAMLET.

It was actually used onstage by David Tennant in 2008.

24. A MAJORITY OF WOODSTOCK'S AUDIENCE MISSED JIMI HENDRIX'S SET.

He took the stage at 9:00 am, as the last act of the festival, but about 300,000 of the half-million people there had already left or were leaving.

25. FINLAND HAS MORE HEAVY METAL BANDS PER CAPITA THAN ANY OTHER COUNTRY.

Must be all the snow.

26. THERE WAS A NON-EXISTENT COMPOSER IN THE PRESTIGIOUS THE NEW GROVE DICTIONARY OF MUSIC AND MUSICIANS.

Dag Henrik Esrum-Hellerup (named after railway stops in Copenhagen) was said to be a nineteenth-century Danish composer. The writer of the entry made him up as a joke and didn't think the editors would let it slip through. They did, and the entry wasn't removed until after 1980.

27. BARRY MANILOW DIDN'T ACTUALLY WRITE THE SONG CALLED "I WRITE THE SONGS."

It may be his most famous song, but he didn't write it. It was composed by Bruce Johnston of the Beach Boys. To be fair, Manilow was reluctant to record it at first, because the words make it seem pretty egotistical.

28. METALLICA HAS PERFORMED ON ALL SEVEN CONTINENTS.

Not only that, they did it in one year, 2013.

· 29 ·

ELVIS PRESLEY'S GRACELAND IS THE SECOND MOST VISITED PRIVATE HOME IN THE UNITED STATES, AFTER THE WHITE HOUSE.

30. MUSIC, ALONG WITH LITERATURE, ARCHITECTURE, PAINTING, AND SCULPTURE WERE OLYMPIC EVENTS FROM 1912 UNTIL 1948.

The only reason these competitions stopped was because the Olympic committee decided that they were professional occupations and at the time all competitors had to be amateurs.

31. IN 2016, WOLFGANG AMADEUS MOZART SOLD MORE CDS THAN BEYONCÉ.

Okay, this one is a bit of a trick. That year, a boxed set of his complete works appeared, containing 200(!) CDs. So it only needed to sell just over 6,200 copies to become the year's best-seller, since Billboard counts each CD in the set as an individual sale.

32. EXPERIMENTAL COMPOSER JOHN CAGE WROTE A PIECE DURING WHICH THE PERFORMER DOES NOTHING FOR FOUR MINUTES AND THIRTY-THREE SECONDS.

Called "4'33," the idea is to let the natural sounds of the room, concert hall, outdoors, etc., provide the "music." Many interpretations exist.

33. IN THE 1980S, THERE WERE MORE PEOPLE IN MONACO'S ORCHESTRA THAN IN ITS ARMY.

Eighty-five and eighty, to be exact, but this is no longer the case. The military now has over 250 people, and very few orchestras need to be that big!

34. THE NAMESAKE OF THE FENDER GUITAR DIDN'T KNOW HOW TO PLAY GUITAR.

Leo Fender, who founded the Fender Electric Instruments, was an innovative inventor who changed popular music, but the only instruments he knew how to play were piano and saxophone (and neither one very well).

35. GREECE'S NATIONAL ANTHEM IS 158 VERSES LONG.

Imagine memorizing all of those!

36. TERMITES EAT WOOD TWICE AS QUICKLY WHEN EXPOSED TO HEAVY METAL.

Heavy wood?

37. SONGS BY TINA TURNER WERE USED AT GLOUCESTERSHIRE AIRPORT IN ENGLAND TO SCARE BIRDS AWAY FROM THE RUNWAY.

The usual distress sounds weren't working, so they happened to turn on a recording and it was hers. Apparently, it was successful.

38. THE JAPANESE NATIONAL ANTHEM, "KIMIGAYO," ONLY HAS FOUR LINES OF TEXT.

It's the world's shortest national anthem.

• 39 •

THE TUNE "HAPPY BIRTHDAY" WAS THE FIRST SONG EVER PLAYED ON ANOTHER PLANET.

At the first-year anniversary of the Curiosity rover landing on Mars, it played the song to itself. That's kind of sad, when you think about it.

40. THE VAN HALEN BROTHERS BOTH TRAINED AS CONCERT PIANISTS AS CHILDREN.

In addition, Alex started on guitar and Eddie began on drums, but they switched later.

41. THE CLASSIC FILM *MONTY PYTHON AND THE HOLY GRAIL* WAS FUNDED IN PART BY MEMBERS OF THE ROCK BANDS LED ZEPPELIN AND PINK FLOYD.

They were big fans.

42. THE EQUALLY CLASSIC FILM *MONTY PYTHON'S LIFE OF BRIAN* WAS PARTIALLY FUNDED BY GEORGE HARRISON, FORMERLY OF THE BEATLES.

The film ran out of money during production and Harrison stepped in to provide some needed cash. As a result, he has a small cameo in the movie.

43. THE GUNS N' ROSES'S SONG "SWEET CHILD O' MINE" WAS WRITTEN IN FIVE MINUTES.

According to bass player Duff McKagan, guitarist Slash was messing around with an exercise and the others liked it and put something together very quickly. Slash later said it was the band's worst song.

44. ALFRED HITCHCOCK ORIGINALLY DIDN'T WANT MUSIC IN *PSYCHO'S* FAMOUS SHOWER SCENE.

He changed his mind after hearing the proposed music and raised composer Bernard Herrmann's salary. Can you imagine that scene without the screeching strings?

45. CLASSICAL AND HEAVY METAL MUSIC ATTRACT FANS WITH SIMILAR PERSONALITIES BUT WITH DIFFERENT AGES.

That might also explain why so many metal bands use classical themes and ideas in their songs.

46. RETAILERS OFTEN PLAY SLOW MUSIC TO KEEP YOU IN THE STORE SO YOU'LL BUY MORE.

In less fancy restaurants, faster music is played to encourage a rapid turnover.

47. THE MUSIC FOR "THE STAR-SPANGLED BANNER" COMES FROM A BRITISH DRINKING SONG.

Known as "To Anacreon in Heaven," it was a popular song sung in a British drinking club, the Anacreontic Society. The tune was dedicated to the ancient Greek poet Anacreon (also known for writing drinking songs), inviting him to be their patron, and it was sung after meetings, when the fun part of the evening began. The adaptation to Francis Scott Key's words came later.

· 48 ·

RESEARCHERS AT THE UNIVERSITY OF LEICESTER IN ENGLAND DISCOVERED THAT COWS PRODUCE 3% MORE MILK WHEN LISTENING TO RELAXING MUSIC.

In the same study, rap and techno did not improve their milk output. Make of it what you will.

49. NINETEENTH-CENTURY COMPOSER FRANZ LISZT SENT DOG HAIRS TO HIS FANS.

He had so many requests for locks of his hair that he finally bought a dog and snipped off small bits of its fur to send to his fans.

50. ZILDJIAN HAS BEEN MAKING CYMBALS SINCE THE ZENITH OF THE OTTOMAN EMPIRE IN 1623.

The company's cymbals are now used in drum kits around the world, but at first they made loud cymbals used by the Ottoman Turkish army to scare their enemies.

51. THE FAMED LONDON SYMPHONY ORCHESTRA WAS ORIGINALLY BOOKED TO SAIL ON THE *TITANIC* ON ITS DOOMED MAIDEN VOYAGE.

The orchestra ended up on another ship a week earlier, however. They really dodged a bullet, er, iceberg.

52. THE BEATLES SONG "YESTERDAY" WAS ORIGINALLY CALLED "SCRAMBLED EGGS."

It was just a working title, thankfully: "Scrambled eggs… all my hunger seems so far away." Doesn't really work, does it?

53. FRANK BEARD IS THE ONLY MEMBER OF THE ROCK BAND ZZ TOP THAT DOESN'T HAVE A BEARD.

54. ELVIS PRESLEY NEVER PERFORMED OUTSIDE OF THE UNITED STATES OR CANADA.

And he only ever did five shows in Canada, on a short tour.

55. THE BEATLES WERE ONCE CALLED JOHNNY AND THE MOONDOGS.

They also tried out the Quarrymen and The Silver Beetles.

56. "JINGLE BELLS" WAS ORIGINALLY WRITTEN FOR THANKSGIVING.

The composer, James Lord Pierpont, wanted a little tune for his students to sing at the Thanksgiving holiday in 1850 or 1851. It was a hit, and soon after, it started being sung for Christmas, too.

57. THE OLDEST SURVIVING PIECE OF MUSIC WE CAN READ DATES FROM ABOUT 1400 BCE.

Known as the "Hurrian Hymn to Nikkal" (an orchard goddess), it comes from what is now northern Syria. The musical notation isn't completely clear, so there are several different versions of what it may sound like.

• 58 •

NIRVANA WAS KICKED OUT
OF THE RELEASE PARTY FOR
THEIR ALBUM *NEVERMIND*
FOR STARTING A FOOD FIGHT.

59. JOHANN SEBASTIAN BACH FATHERED TWENTY CHILDREN BY TWO WIVES.

Even in the days when having many children was the norm, this seems like a lot! Sadly, only ten of them survived to adulthood, a very common occurrence.

60. CHUCK BERRY REALLY WANTED TO BE A PHOTOGRAPHER.

Early on, he mainly performed music to make money to buy more photography equipment. He also trained as a carpenter and hairdresser.

61. TRUE OR FALSE? THE BRITISH NAVY ONCE USED BRITNEY SPEARS SONGS TO SCARE OFF PIRATES.

True. The navy discovered that pirates from Somalia hated her music and the Western culture it came from, so they stayed away from ships blasting it out loud.

62. TRUE OR FALSE? THE HARMONICA IS PROBABLY THE WORLD'S BEST-SELLING MUSICAL INSTRUMENT.

True. It's small, portable, and pretty easy to learn, so that makes sense. The double bass, on the other hand...

63. TRUE OR FALSE? NONE OF THE MEMBERS OF THE BEATLES COULD READ MUSIC.

True. This isn't all that uncommon for pop and rock bands, but given the quality of their musical output, it is kind of remarkable.

64. TRUE OR FALSE? AS OF 2019, THE BEATLES HAVE SOLD OVER 100 MILLION ALBUMS.

False. They've actually sold over 183 million albums, more than the Rolling Stones and Led Zeppelin combined.

65. TRUE OR FALSE? ROLLING STONES VOCALIST MICK JAGGER IS AN AVID BALLET DANCER.

True. He has long used it as part of his fitness routine.

66. TRUE OR FALSE? LOUD MUSIC DECREASES THE SPEED OF DRINKING AND THE AMOUNT OF ALCOHOL THAT PEOPLE DRINK AT BARS.

False. It actually increases the speed.

67. TRUE OR FALSE? KENYAN MUSICIANS SOMETIMES MUST PLAY THEIR GIGS WHILE THEY ARE LOCKED INSIDE METAL CAGES!

True. Many musicians can't afford their own instruments, so nightclubs provide them, but make the musicians play from locked areas to prevent theft

· 68 ·

TRUE OR FALSE? THERE IS AN ORCHESTRA THAT USES INSTRUMENTS MADE OF VEGETABLES.

True. Based in Vienna, they make instruments like drums and flutes out of veggies, and even put the leftover parts into soups to be served to audiences!

69. TRUE OR FALSE? AT SOME WEDDINGS IN NORTHERN INDIA, THERE ARE GROUPS OF WOMEN WHO SING "ABUSE" SONGS FULL OF PROFANITY TO FAMILY OF THE GROOM.

True. Known as a "gali", this type of song is meant as a joke, and a sign of affection.

70. TRUE OR FALSE? THE AINU PEOPLE OF THE ISLANDS NORTH OF JAPAN USED TO ENTERTAIN EACH OTHER BY SINGING INTO EACH OTHER'S EARS.

False. They actually sang into each other's mouths.

71. TRUE OR FALSE? THE BEATLES TRIED OUT FOR DECCA RECORDS IN 1962, BUT THEY WERE TURNED DOWN.

True. They were told that "groups of guitars are on the way out." The Decca execs probably felt very stupid a few years later.

72. TRUE OR FALSE? THERE IS A LARGE ORGAN PLAYED BY THE SEA.

True. It's in the city of Zadar, Croatia. Concealed under marble steps leading down to the water are a series of polyethylene tubes and a large resonating chamber. When waves and wind hit these tubes, different notes sound. It's an instrument played entirely by nature.

73. TRUE OR FALSE? IN 1965, CHARLES MANSON AUDITIONED TO BE A MEMBER OF THE MONKEES.

False. Though he had a talent for music, he was in prison at the time.

74. TRUE OR FALSE? ELVIS PRESLEY WAS SECRETLY A U.S. FEDERAL AGENT.

False. In 1970, he approached President Richard Nixon about becoming a "federal agent at large," and Nixon even got him a badge, but nothing more seems to have come of it.

75. TRUE OR FALSE? DISTORTED GUITAR TONE, COMMON IN ROCK MUSIC, ORIGINATED WITH COUNTRY MUSIC.

True, sort of. In 1961, country guitarist Grady Martin played with a faulty amplifier and liked the tone, so he started using what became known as the "fuzz effect." Other musicians had experimented with raw sounds before, but his was the one that stuck.

76. TRUE OR FALSE? QUEEN GUITARIST BRIAN MAY IS ALSO A MEDICAL DOCTOR.

False. He's an astrophysicist with a Ph.D. in the subject.

• 77 •

TRUE OR FALSE? SHARKS LIKE HEAVY METAL.

False. An Australian study found that they actually like jazz.

78. TRUE OR FALSE? THE BAND DEPECHE MODE IS NAMED AFTER A FRENCH MAGAZINE.

True. It means "Fashion Update."

79. TRUE OR FALSE? DUKE ELLINGTON LOVED THE COLOR GREEN SO MUCH HE ALWAYS HAD TO WEAR IT.

False. He actually hated grass (it reminded him of cemeteries) and the color green in general. He wouldn't even have garments in his wardrobe that were green.

80. TRUE OR FALSE? BEETHOVEN RIGOROUSLY COUNTED HIS COFFEE BEANS, TO MAKE SURE THAT HE ALWAYS HAD THE SAME AMOUNT IN EVERY CUP.

True. Maybe he just wanted his drink to taste the same every time?

81. TRUE OR FALSE? JOHN LENNON HATED THE SOUND OF HIS OWN VOICE.

True. He even asked his producer: "Can't you smother it with tomato ketchup or something?"

82. TRUE OR FALSE? JOHNNY CASH RECORDED A LIVE CONCERT ALBUM IN SAN QUENTIN PRISON.

True. It was in 1969.

83. TRUE OR FALSE? SWISS CHEESE DEVELOPS A STRONGER FLAVOR WHILE AGING WHEN IT'S EXPOSED TO CLASSIC ROCK.

False. It actually gets stronger when exposed to hip-hop.

84. TRUE OR FALSE? JIMI HENDRIX WAS ONCE THE OPENING ACT FOR THE MONKEES.

True. He wasn't thrilled with the idea, and it only lasted for seven shows in 1967.

• 85 •

TRUE OR FALSE? MOZART SOMETIMES PRETENDED TO BE A CAT.

True. He was known to sometimes meow, jump over furniture, and do somersaults. Some think he may have had Tourette's Syndrome, since he showed off a number of other unorthodox behaviors.

Science

Science is "sciencey" and should be reliable, right? Well, yes, but at the same time, some of the weirdest facts out there come from various scientific fields. This is especially true when you get into subjects like quantum physics, where reality breaks down and seems to make no sense (our atoms are mostly empty space and things only potentially exist, for example). But there are plenty of other strange facts to be found in biology, chemistry, earth science, and more. Here is a sampling of some of the more unusual ones.

1. LUNA MOTHS DON'T HAVE MOUTHS, OR A DIGESTIVE SYSTEM.

They only live for about seven days, during which time they mate and then die, so they have no need to eat anything.

2. WHEN POURED, HOT WATER AND COLD WATER SOUND DIFFERENT.

Hot water has a higher pitched sound because the molecules are moving faster. People can generally tell when hot or cold water is being poured, if they are not looking.

3. HUMANS HAVE MORE THAN FIVE SENSES.

We actually have between fourteen and twenty, including sense of balance, sense of space, sense of time, detecting temperature, and sense of movement.

4. SOME SHARKS CAN CARRY THEIR YOUNG FOR AS LONG THREE YEARS.

The basking shark has a gestation period of three years, while other sharks, such as the spiny dogfish shark, have pregnancies that last two years or more.

· 5 ·

SUNFLOWERS CAN BE USED
TO CLEAN UP NUCLEAR
WASTE AND RADIOACTIVE
CONTAMINANTS FROM SOIL.
THEY SOAK UP RADIOACTIVE
ISOTOPES, DRAWING
RADIATION OUT OF SOIL.

6. THE BOMBARDIER BEETLE EXCRETES BOILING HOT LIQUID.

To fend off predators, this beetle can shoot a hot chemical mixture of hydroquinone and hydrogen peroxide. These are contained in separate places in the beetle's abdomen until it needs to use them.

7. OVER THE COURSE OF AN AVERAGE HUMAN LIFE SPAN, THE MOUTH PRODUCES ENOUGH SALIVA TO FILL 53 BATHTUBS.

That's about two tablespoons per day.

8. OUR EARS AND NOSES KEEP ON GROWING THROUGHOUT OUR WHOLE LIVES.

9. TWELVE PLANTS AND FIVE ANIMAL SPECIES ARE THE SOURCE OF 75% OF THE WORLD'S FOOD.

There are between 250,000 to 300,000 known edible plant species, but humans only use 150 to 200 of them.

10. TOBACCO SMOKE ENEMAS WERE ONCE GIVEN TO RESUSCITATE DROWNING VICTIMS.

Believe it or not, a woman who had apparently drowned was revived by this method in 1746. The practice survived into the nineteenth century.

11. BABIES ARE BORN WITH ABOUT 300 BONES, BUT ADULTS ONLY HAVE 206.

This is because certain bones fuse together as we grow, and some are made only of cartilage, so that by adulthood the total number has gone way down.

12. ALL THE MATTER THAT MAKES UP THE HUMAN RACE COULD FIT IN A SUGAR CUBE, IF ONE COULD REMOVE ALL THE EMPTY SPACE IN OUR ATOMS.

Atoms are 99.9999999% (or more) empty space.

13. THERE'S NO LETTER "J" ON THE PERIODIC TABLE.

Go and have a look.

14. LEAFCUTTER ANTS CAN CARRY OBJECTS UP TO FIFTY TIMES THEIR OWN BODY WEIGHT.

And they do it only using their jaws. For a human, this would be like being able to lift a car with your teeth.

15. THE UNITED KINGDOM HAS THE MOST TORNADOES PER SQUARE MILE.

Not Kansas, not Oklahoma. Maybe the Wizard of Oz should have been set in Yorkshire?

• 16 •

GRASSHOPPERS' EARS ARE ON THEIR STOMACHS.

They have membranes—known as the tympanum—that vibrate and detect sound, and are located on its first abdominal segment.

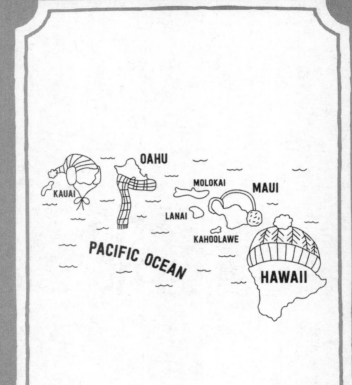

KAUAI

OAHU

MOLOKAI

MAUI

LANAI

KAHOOLAWE

PACIFIC OCEAN

HAWAII

· 17 ·

HAWAII MOVES ALMOST THREE INCHES CLOSER TO ALASKA EVERY YEAR.

This is due to plate tectonics. The Hawaiian Islands sit on the Pacific Tectonic Plate, which is moving northwest at the speed of about three or four miles an hour. A new island south of the Big Island is also being formed by volcanic activity, and will pop up out of the waves thousands of years from now.

18. GLASS IS NOT A LIQUID OR A SOLID.

It's classified as an amorphous solid, which means that its molecules are moving, just very slowly and imperceptibly.

19. BABIES ARE BORN CRYING WITH AN ACCENT.

They may be trying to imitate outside sounds they hear in the womb. One study showed that German and French newborns cried differently, for example. This may also help with mother-child bonding.

20. THE PRESENT CAN AFFECT WHAT HAPPENED IN THE PAST.

The idea comes from the weird world of quantum physics, and is known as "retrocausality." It's not proven, but it suggests that a subatomic particle might be able to move backward through time to when it was entangled with another particle and affect that other. It's a head-scratcher, that's for sure!

21. THE EIFFEL TOWER IS UP TO SIX INCHES TALLER DURING THE SUMMER.

Heat makes the metal at the base of the tower expand, pushing it up slightly. Not that you'd ever really notice.

22. EVERY SECOND, ABOUT 100 BILLION SOLAR NEUTRINOS PASS THROUGH EVERY INCH OF YOUR BODY, AND YOU NEVER EVEN NOTICE.

These subatomic particles originate in the sun and are so small that you couldn't possibly see them, even in the billions.

23. IT TAKES ABOUT FIFTY PAIRS OF MUSCLES TO CHEW AND SWALLOW A SINGLE BITE OF FOOD.

24. KILLER WHALES ARE ACTUALLY DOLPHINS.

25. PHOBIAS MAY BE CAUSED BY MEMORIES PASSED DOWN THROUGH THE GENES FROM OUR ANCESTORS.

New studies suggest that memories can be "inherited," due to actual chemical changes in one's DNA over the course of a life. It may be an evolutionary safety adaptation.

26. THERE'S A TYPE OF FUNGUS CALLED CHORIOACTIS THAT IS FOUND IN ONLY TWO PLACES ON EARTH: PARTS OF CENTRAL AND NORTHEAST TEXAS, AND IN SOUTHERN JAPAN.

No one is quite sure why.

• 27 •

GIRAFFE TONGUES HAVE A NATURAL SUNSCREEN.

Their tongues are very long and black toward the end. This is due to having more melanin (which gives skin its darker color), a handy evolutionary adaptation that protects the delicate tongue from getting sunburned while reaching into treetops to get food.

• 28 •

A HIPPOPOTAMUS CAN RUN FASTER THAN A HUMAN.

Despite their enormous size, hippos can run as fast as thirty miles per hour, far faster than a human.

29. A COCKROACH CAN SURVIVE FOR MORE THAN A WEEK WITHOUT ITS HEAD.

They don't need the head to breathe, the wound will sometimes just seal up, and while they will eventually dehydrate, their last meal can sustain them for some time. Gross!

30. VULTURE BEES EAT ROTTING CARCASSES INSTEAD OF NECTAR.

They then store that meat in their stomach and vomit it out later to make a kind of "meat honey."

31. BANANAS ARE RADIOACTIVE.

They get it mainly from their potassium content, but the amount is so small you'd have to consume about a hundred bananas per day to even get the equivalent of your daily exposure to radiation. Actually, lots of fruits are also radioactive, so it's no big deal. Eat your bananas!

32. NO ONE KNOWS WHY WE HAVE TO SLEEP.

33. POLAR BEARS ARE ALMOST INVISIBLE TO INFRARED CAMERAS.

Infrared cameras detect heat signatures, but the bears have such good insulation from their fur and a thick layer of fat that very little heat escapes their bodies. Thus, infrared cameras can't easily spot them.

34. HOT WATER FREEZES FASTER THAN COLD WATER.

This seems to be due to the Mpemba effect, which states that water molecules in faster motion are predisposed to freeze more quickly.

35. ON THE OTHER HAND, COLD WATER ACTUALLY GETS HOT FASTER THAN WARM WATER.

Again, the Mpemba effect shows that the opposite is also true; molecule activity is at play here.

36. EACH PERSON'S TONGUE MARKINGS ARE UNIQUE, JUST LIKE THEIR FINGERPRINTS.

37. A STARFISH HAS NO BRAIN OR BLOOD.

It has a nervous system, and eyes, and pumps sea water through its system as a substitute.

38. GALLIUM IS A METAL THAT CAN MELT IN YOUR HAND.

It has a melting temperature of 85.6°F, and is safe to handle.

39. THE GALAPAGOS TORTOISE CAN LIVE TO BE WELL OVER 100 YEARS OLD.

Some have lived to be 200.

· 40 ·

**RATS LAUGH WHEN
THEY'RE TICKLED.**

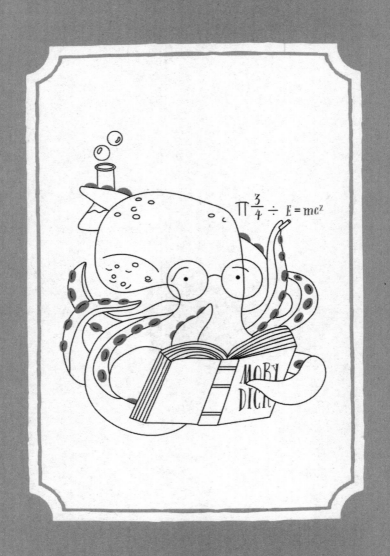

• 41 •

THE GIANT PACIFIC OCTOPUS HAS NINE BRAINS.

One is a central brain, with a smaller brain in each arm that helps control its movement.

• 42 •

FLAMINGOES ARE ACTUALLY WHITE.

It's the food they eat (brine shrimp that eat certain algae) that turns them pink.

43. A FINNISH PINE TREE CAN HAVE MORE THAN THIRTY MILES OF ROOTS.

44. AN ICE CUBE HAS ABOUT 9% MORE VOLUME THAN THE WATER DID BEFORE IT FROZE.

This is because water expands as it freezes, unlike most liquids.

45. THE HUMAN BODY IS MADE UP OF ABOUT SEVEN OCTILLION ATOMS.

That's seven followed by twenty-seven zeros.

46. ACCORDING TO QUANTUM PHYSICS, OBJECTIVE REALITY MAY NOT EXIST.

At the quantum level, when you observe a system, it chooses a specific state or location, but normally, particles can be in different states or locations at the same time, which is known as superposition. Makes your head hurt thinking about it, doesn't it?

47. TERMITES SPEND A LOT TIME GROOMING EACH OTHER.

It helps reduce bacteria, parasites, and other nasty things from infesting the colony. Presumably, they do this when not eating your house.

48. IF ALL OF THE DNA IN YOUR BODY WERE LINED UP, IT WOULD COVER THE DISTANCE FROM THE EARTH TO THE SUN AND BACK 600 TIMES.

We're really complex creatures.

49. ONE TEASPOON OF WATER CONTAINS ABOUT THREE TIMES AS MANY ATOMS AS THERE ARE TEASPOONS OF WATER IN THE ATLANTIC OCEAN.

Atoms are very small!

50. FEMALE KOMODO DRAGONS CAN PRODUCE OFFSPRING WITHOUT CONTACT FROM MALES.

It's done through a process called "parthenogenesis," which has been observed in dozens of species, especially reptiles. It may be a survival adaptation for when dragon dudes are not around.

51. THERE ARE MORE BACTERIA IN A HUMAN MOUTH THAN THERE ARE HUMAN BEINGS IN THE WORLD.

Twenty billion on average, compared to a human population of over seven billion. That number goes way up if you don't brush your teeth for a day.

• 52 •

THERE WERE ONCE PENGUINS AS TALL AS HUMANS.

They lived between 66 and 56 million years ago, in what became New Zealand. They could stand 5'3" in height and weigh over 170 pounds.

53. SINCE ITS DISCOVERY IN 1930, PLUTO HAS NOT YET MADE A COMPLETE ORBIT OF THE SUN.

Its orbit takes 248 Earth years, so it won't be in the same place again until 2178.

54. MALE GIRAFFES TASTE THE PEE OF FEMALES TO FIND OUT IF THEY ARE READY TO MATE.

The males (bulls) go about sniffing the females' behinds, hoping to get a squirt of pee, which will contain hormones indicating they are ready to mate. You probably didn't need to know this.

55. THE HUMAN BRAIN PRODUCES ENOUGH ELECTRICITY TO POWER A LIGHT BULB.

All of your neurons together produce enough electricity to do it. Maybe this is where the light bulb appearing over someone's head when they have a good idea came from?

56. THE MOON USED TO HAVE AN ATMOSPHERE.

About three to four billion years ago, it had volcanoes that erupted gas too quickly to be lost to space. The atmosphere lasted about seven million years.

57. WATER WOULD BOIL IN A GLASS EXPOSED TO THE VACUUM OF SPACE.

Water boils when there is no pressure, but the water vapor would quickly begin to freeze.

58. BEES CAN UNDERSTAND THE CONCEPT OF ZERO.

Studies have shown that bees can be trained to understand that the lack of a number is a number. They were rewarded with a drop of sweet water when they flew to a card with fewer objects on it, but when the objects were taken away, they still went to that same card, showing that they understand how nothing is less than something.

59. A VOLCANO IN GUATEMALA, KNOWN AS SANTA MARIA, HAS BEEN ERUPTING ALMOST EVERY HOUR FOR OVER NINETY-FOUR YEARS.

Scientists are still figuring out why, but its regularity is almost unique in the world.

• 60 •

**ANTEATERS CAN EAT 35,000
ANTS PER DAY.**

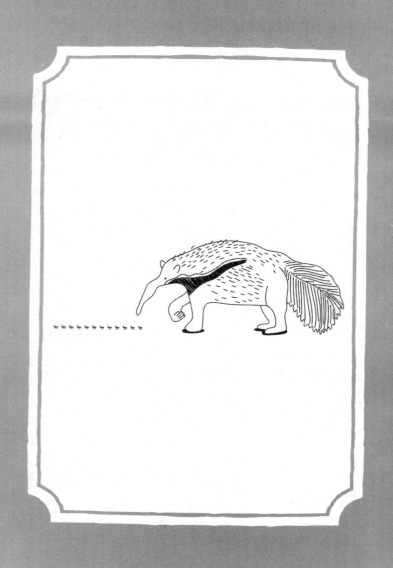

61. **TRUE OR FALSE? SOME SPECIES OF BAMBOO CAN GROW THREE FEET PER DAY.**

True. That's about an inch every forty minutes!

62. **TRUE OR FALSE? A HUMAN ORGAN THAT NO-ONE KNEW ABOUT WAS DISCOVERED IN 2017.**

True. It's called the mesentery, and seems to help with various bodily functions, including the immune system.

63. **TRUE OR FALSE? DUNG BEETLES NAVIGATE BY USING THE MILKY WAY.**

True. Amazingly, the little insects use the strip of light in the night sky to move in a straight line relative to it.

64. **TRUE OR FALSE? HYENAS ARE MORE CLOSELY RELATED TO CATS THAN TO DOGS.**

True. They are a part of the family Hyaenidae, which is in the suborder Feliformia, which also includes cats.

65. **TRUE OR FALSE? HUMANS SHARE 50% OF THEIR DNA WITH BANANAS.**

False. We actually share 50% of our genes with bananas, which is only about 1% of our DNA.

66. TRUE OR FALSE? WHITE IS NOT ACTUALLY A COLOR.

True. It's the absence of color. But white light is all lights combined.

67. TRUE OR FALSE? MOST HOUSE DUST IS HUMAN SKIN.

True. Makes you feel a bit itchy, doesn't it?

68. TRUE OR FALSE? WE CAN'T TASTE FOOD WITHOUT SALIVA.

True. Saliva helps dissolve food. The enzymes in it break down food structures and help release molecules in food that your taste buds can detect.

69. TRUE OR FALSE? ABOUT 1% OF THE HUMAN GENOME MAY COME FROM PLANTS.

True. It may have happened by a process known as horizontal gene transfer, in which bacteria can share genetic information. So we're all just a bit plant!

70. TRUE OR FALSE? THERE ARE OVER 300 TYPES OF ICE.

True. More than 300 different kinds of molecular arrangements, to be exact, but most only exist at very low temperatures, so they would only be found on other planets.

• 71 •

TRUE OR FALSE? ON SOME PLANETS, IT RAINS DIAMONDS.

True. Scientists believe that Saturn, Uranus, and Neptune have the atmospheric and pressure conditions, as well as abundant carbon, to make diamond rains possible.

72. TRUE OR FALSE? YOUR APPENDIX HAS NO PURPOSE IN THE BODY.

False. Recent research suggests that it helps the immune system and provides a place to store helpful gut bacteria.

73. TRUE OR FALSE? THERE MAY BE BLACK HOLES THE SIZE OF ONLY ONE ATOM.

True. They are theoretical and may act differently than "regular" black holes, but they might pass through the Earth every day!

74. TRUE OR FALSE? THE SUN LOSES ABOUT 5.5 MILLION TONS OF ITS MASS EVERY SECOND.

True. This is due to both the sun generating the solar wind (ionized particles) and because of its nuclear fusion, which expels energy in the form of light and heat. Don't worry, though. Given the sun's size, this is a negligible amount.

75. TRUE OR FALSE? THERE ARE MORE MICROORGANISMS IN A SINGLE TEASPOON OF SOIL THAN THERE ARE PEOPLE ON EARTH.

True. There are billions of bacteria, algae, and other microscopic life forms.

76. TRUE OR FALSE? YOUR STOMACH TAKES SEVEN YEARS TO DIGEST CHEWING GUM.

False. This is a silly old urban legend that is not true.

77. TRUE OR FALSE? FLEAS CAN ACCELERATE FASTER WHEN THEY JUMP THAN THE SPACE SHUTTLE.

True. In fact, their acceleration is about a hundred times the force of gravity!

78. TRUE OR FALSE? WATER CAN EXIST AS A GAS, LIQUID, AND SOLID AT THE SAME TIME.

True. It's at the temperature called the triple point (for water, this is 0.01°C). Think of when ice is melting outside; you can see it as solid, liquid, and sometimes gas all at once.

79. TRUE OR FALSE? LIGHTNING CAN ONLY STRIKE A PLACE ONCE.

False. In the United States alone, there are over twenty million lightning strikes per year. So the chances of lightning hitting the same location more than once are actually quite good. There are also people who have been struck multiple times by lightning!

• 80 •

TRUE OR FALSE? 60,000 JELLYFISH ONCE ORBITED THE EARTH.

True. In 1991, the Space Shuttle Columbia took over 2,000 jellies into orbit as part of an experiment. By the end of the mission, they had reproduced enough to number 60,000!

81. TRUE OR FALSE? BLOOD IS BLUE, AND TURNS RED WITH OXYGEN.

False. Blood contains hemoglobin, which contains iron, which in this case, reflects red when bound to oxygen. You may think some of your veins look blue, but that's not due to the blood in them.

82. TRUE OR FALSE? THE HUMAN STOMACH CAN DISSOLVE RAZOR BLADES.

True. The PH level in the stomach ranges from about 1-3, and the hydrochloric acid is more than enough to dissolve certain metals. We don't recommend trying it out, though.

83. TRUE OR FALSE? FLUSHED TOILETS ROTATE IN OPPOSITE DIRECTIONS IN THE NORTHERN AND SOUTHERN HEMISPHERES, DUE TO THE CORIOLIS EFFECT.

False. The Coriolis Effect is real, but it doesn't affect toilets.

84. TRUE OR FALSE? IT'S NOT POSSIBLE TO BURP IN SPACE.

True. The lack of gravity in space means that air doesn't get separated from food in the stomach, so an attempted burp would probably be more like vomiting.

85. TRUE OR FALSE? FEMALE SHARKS HAVE THICKER SKINS THAN MALES.

True. They evolved thicker skins to protect them from aggressive males when mating.

Entertainment

ENTERTAINMENT FACTS CAN BE
STRANGELY ENTERTAINING

We've been entertaining ourselves since the good old days of painting on cave walls. Beyond music, we've invented drama, dancing, games, television, movies, and, worst of all, the internet, all in an effort to keep ourselves amused and distracted. So, it only stands to reason that some pretty weird stories and facts would emerge from our long history of creative diversions. From Shakespeare to social media, from tragedy to television, here are some truths that may well surprise you.

1. THE PREMIERE OF IGOR STRAVINSKY'S *RITE OF SPRING* IN 1913 SPARKED A RIOT.

Its harsh, dissonant music and angular dancing were unlike anything seen before on a ballet stage. A group of avant-garde enthusiasts were there, in contrast to ballet traditionalists; people were either thrilled or horrified. Descriptions vary, but there are reports of the audience jeering, whistling, throwing things, and even resorting to fisticuffs. Some reports say about forty people were ejected, maybe with the aid of the police. Things calmed down for the second act, and the ballet did receive enthusiastic applause at its conclusion.

2. A RENAISSANCE PLAY ONCE LASTED 30 DAYS.

A monk named Simon Gréban wrote a play based on the Acts of the Apostles in the 1470s. It had over 60,000 lines and a cast of about 500 actors. It was performed a few times, but once in 1539, the production was reported as lasting for a month. Take that, Hollywood blockbusters!

3. AN ENGLISH PLAY MAY HAVE ACCIDENTALLY INSPIRED THE AMERICAN REVOLUTION.

English playwright Joseph Addison wrote a play in 1712 called *Cato, A Tragedy*, about an opponent of Julius Caesar and his tyranny. It caught on in the American colonies, and later, revolutionists such as Patrick Henry and George Washington were inspired by it, quoted it, and even used some of its military tactics.

4. FAMED ACTOR JOHN BARRYMORE NEVER MEMORIZED HIS LINES BEFORE FILMING.

He claimed that his memory was already full of texts from his stage work and that he wouldn't fill his head with "horsesh*t" from the movies he was in. So he demanded that crew members hold up cards with his lines written on them, so he could read them out while filming them.

5. THE LONDON COLISEUM STAGED A HORSE RACE INDOORS IN 1904, WITH REAL HORSES AND RIDERS.

They ran on a carousel-like machine so they stayed stationary while the carousel went round and round in circles. Except that one of the horses stumbled and fell into the orchestra pit, injuring several musicians and killing the jockey. The producers never attempted this spectacle again, by the way.

• 6 •

THE ANCIENT GREEK PLAYWRIGHT AESCHYLUS DIED WHEN AN EAGLE DROPPED A TORTOISE ON HIS HEAD.

More of a legend, the story says that the great author of tragedies was outside when a certain bird of prey mistook his bald head for a rock to bash open the tortoise with. The result was a different kind of tragedy for Aeschylus.

· 7 ·

SHAKESPEARE'S ORIGINAL GLOBE THEATRE BURNED DOWN BECAUSE OF A MISFIRING CANNON ACCIDENT.

Props were strange things in early modern theater, and real guns and canons were sometimes used. During a performance of Shakespeare's *Henry VIII* in 1613, a theater cannon misfired and some of the wooden beams and thatch caught on fire. The whole building burned to the ground.

8. SHAKESPEARE COINED HUNDREDS OF WORDS AND PHRASES THAT WE STILL USE.

Addiction, assassination, eyeball, fashionable, manager, uncomfortable, break the ice, heart of gold, wild-goose chase, laughing stock, for goodness' sake, one fell swoop, knock knock... and so many more!

9. SHAKESPEARE'S HEAD SEEMS TO BE MISSING.

Reports that his skull had been stolen from Holy Trinity church in Stratford date back to the nineteenth century, but a recent radar scan of his grave showed a brick structure where his skull should be, meaning that someone might well have removed it. His grave, incidentally, curses anyone who would dare disturb the Bard's bones, so who knows the fate of the thief?

10. A FRENCH KING USED BALLET TO KEEP HIS COURT UNDER CONTROL.

Louis XIV was completely in love with ballet, and also realized it was a good way to keep his scheming nobles in check. He required them to learn complex dance routines and made them stand in various positions according to rank, basically choreographing their movements. The idea was that they would be so preoccupied with protocol that they wouldn't have time to plot against him.

11. A THEATER COMPANY MANAGER ONCE WALKED INTO A DRESSING ROOM OF BONES.

Nineteenth-century manager Solomon Smith had an interesting discovery in Mississippi. A theater was built near a graveyard and tons of bones had been displaced and thrown in the dressing rooms. One room even featured a skull with a candle in each eye socket.

12. A GAME SHOW GUEST WITNESSED THE ASSASSINATION OF ABRAHAM LINCOLN.

In 1956, 95-year-old Samuel J. Seymour was a guest on the game show *I've Got a Secret*. It turns out that as a very young child he had seen John Wilkes Booth assassinate Abraham Lincoln, though he didn't understand the significance of it at the time. He was the last living witness to a history-changing event.

13. TWO ROMAN DANCERS HAD RIVAL FANS THAT FOUGHT EACH OTHER IN THE STREETS.

Pylades and Bathyllus (late first century BCE) were both dancers of great skill, and hugely popular. The problem was that they were rivals, and their fans became rivals, too, so much so that these crowds often resorted to name-calling and then violence, even riots.

• 14 •

PEACOCK FEATHERS ARE FORBIDDEN IN MOST WESTERN THEATERS.

Theater is plagued with more superstition than perhaps any other profession, and peacock feathers are seen as especially unlucky. The pattern on the top represents the evil eye to some, and to bring one in will curse the production.

15. SHAKESPEARE'S CLOWN ONCE DANCED FROM LONDON TO NORWICH (OVER 100 MILES).

William Kempe was a well-known clown in Shakespeare's acting company, but in 1599 he parted ways with them, seemingly over the usual "artistic differences." In order to keep his name in the spotlight, he hit on a publicity stunt: to dance from London to Norwich in only three weeks. He not only attracted huge crowds, he succeeded!

16. MANY BELIEVE THAT ONE OF SHAKESPEARE'S PLAYS IS CURSED.

Macbeth is a popular tragedy. But one is never supposed to say the title in a theater. Rather you should always call it "The Scottish Play." If someone accidentally does say it, they must recite certain phrases, leave the theater, spin around three times, curse, and then knock to be let back in. And there have been a large number of accidents and mishaps associated with staging the play over the centuries.

17. IN SEVENTEENTH-CENTURY SPAIN, DISPUTES WERE SOMETIMES SETTLED BY DANCING DUELS.

The idea was to minimize injuries and death, so the two opponents would agree on a time and place, judges were present, musicians would be provided, and the duel would begin. The best dancer was declared the winner, and the quarrel was ended.

18. THE WALTZ WAS ONCE A TERRIBLY SCANDALOUS DANCE.

It might seem innocent and old-fashioned now, but the waltz was widely condemned in the nineteenth century. The close proximity between the dancers was something fairly new, and more uptight types didn't like it. Whole books were written about the waltz's evil and corrupting ways.

19. A FAMED NEW YORK SOCIALITE DINNER SEEMS TO HAVE BEEN CURSED.

In 1896, some of P.T. Barnum's family members threw a lavish dinner with an "exotic" dancer. The police got wind of the affair and broke it up, but a huge number of tragedies happened afterward. The dancer died, either from murder or gas poisoning; one of the Barnums was arrested for financial crimes; another killed himself before being arrested for the same reason; Barnum's favorite granddaughter died shortly after; another guest was later bitten on the mouth by his favorite horse and nearly died of blood poisoning. Believe it not, these are only a few of several more.

20. MATA HARI'S HEAD WAS KEPT PRESERVED FOR DECADES AFTER HER EXECUTION.

Famed dancer and spy Mata Hari was executed in 1917, on probably-false charges of being a double agent. Since no one claimed her body, her head was removed and given to the Museum of Anatomy in Paris. It went missing in the 1950s, and no one knows where it is now.

• 21 •

A FAMOUS BALLET DANCER ONCE KILLED A BURGLAR WITH HER FEET.

Nineteenth-century ballet dancer Fanny Essler was sailing to New York when one night a crew member broke into her cabin, intent on stealing her valuable jewelry. She responded with a strong kick to his head, and he died of his injuries a few days later.

22. *THE NUTCRACKER* ONCE HAD A SEVEN-HEADED RAT AND WASN'T ALWAYS SO FAMILY-FRIENDLY.

The original version of the story from 1816 featured Marie (not Clara), who has a series of bizarre dreams and cuts herself badly on a glass cabinet. Oh, and she sees a seven-headed Rat King. Alexander Dumas (of *Three Musketeers* fame) rewrote the story in 1844 to the more familiar version that Tchaikovsky later adapted to his ballet.

23. WALT DISNEY WORLD IN FLORIDA HAS OVER 1.2 MILLION COSTUMES IN ITS WARDROBE.

24. *SNOW WHITE* ORIGINALLY HAD A GRISLY ENDING OF BURNED FEET AND DEADLY DANCING.

In the original Grimm's version, the queen is actually Snow White's mother, and at the end of the story she comes to Snow White's wedding, only to be clamped into iron shoes that have been in a fire. Her feet are horribly burned and she's forced to dance herself to death. Yep, they left that part out of the movie.

25. SHAKESPEARE'S GLOBE (OPENED IN 1997) WAS THE FIRST BUILDING IN LONDON ALLOWED TO HAVE A THATCHED ROOF SINCE THE FIRE IN 1666.

Thatch catches fire very easily, so it was understandable that it would be banned. But in the interest of authenticity, the new Globe was allowed to use it.

26. *THE INTIMATE REVIEW* AT THE DUCHESS THEATRE IN LONDON CLOSED BEFORE THE FIRST PERFORMANCE ENDED.

The play holds the record for the shortest run of a show in West End history. It must have been really bad!

27. WHEN SHAKESPEARE'S GLOBE BURNED IN 1613, ONLY ONE MAN WAS SLIGHTLY INJURED, WHEN HIS BREECHES CAUGHT ON FIRE, BUT HE WAS ABLE TO PUT OUT THE FLAMES WITH ALE.

28. FRENCH COMIC PLAYWRIGHT MOLIÈRE DIED IN 1673 AFTER HE COLLAPSED ON STAGE ACTING IN ONE OF HIS OWN WORKS; HE WAS PLAYING THE ROLE OF A HYPOCHONDRIAC WHO WAS AFRAID OF DEATH AND DOCTORS.

The play was *The Imaginary Invalid*. He'd been sick for some time, and after his collapse he was taken home, where he later died.

29. A "DEUTERAGONIST" IS THE SECOND CHARACTER OR ACTOR IN A STORY AFTER THE PROTAGONIST.

It's first mentioned in a book by G. H. Lewes from 1855, but hardly anyone uses it.

30. THE FIRST EVER YOUTUBE VIDEO FEATURED ELEPHANTS.

In 2005, YouTube co-founder Jawed Karim posted a video of himself at the San Diego Zoo, in front of some elephants, telling us that it's cool that they have long trunks. Not the most profound launch of a website.

31. THERE IS NO ROW "I" IN BROADWAY THEATERS.

This is to prevent confusion about it being row "1" or the front row.

32. TWITTER'S SERVERS CAN HANDLE AND STORE 18 QUINTILLION USERS.

That's 18, followed by eighteen zeros.

33. AT THE END OF THE RUN FOR THEATRICAL PRODUCTIONS, IT'S CONSIDERED GOOD LUCK TO GIVE THE DIRECTOR A BOUQUET OF FLOWERS STOLEN FROM A GRAVE.

34. MICKEY MOUSE HAS A SISTER NAMED FELICITY FIELDMOUSE.

35. DANIEL RADCLIFFE USED ABOUT 160 PAIRS OF GLASSES OVER THE EIGHT FILMS IN WHICH HE PLAYED HARRY POTTER.

He also went through more than sixty wands.

36. THERE ARE NEARLY 400 MILLION TWITTER ACCOUNTS THAT HAVE NO FOLLOWERS.

So why are they even there?

37. THE AVERAGE AMERICAN WILL HAVE SEEN MORE THAN TWO MILLION TELEVISION COMMERCIALS BY THE AGE OF SIXTY-FIVE.

But how many of them have convinced us to actually buy a product?

38. *PSYCHO* WAS THE FIRST FILM IN THE UNITED STATES TO SHOW A TOILET FLUSHING.

It had been considered inappropriate to have onscreen.

• 39 •

THE SNOW SEEN IN *THE WIZARD OF OZ* MOVIE IS MADE OF ASBESTOS.

Talk about occupational hazards!

• 40 •

A FAMOUS BALLET DANCER USED TO TAKE A LEOPARD FOR WALKS ON THE STREETS OF PARIS.

Russian dancer Ida Rubenstein owned a leopard and would walk it on a leash. Apparently, shop keepers who got wind of her comings and goings would close up early because they feared for their safety. Who can blame them?

41. THERE ARE AT LEAST THIRTY MILLION DEAD PEOPLE WITH FACEBOOK ACCOUNTS.

Researchers at Oxford University have estimated that by 2069 there will be more dead users than living ones on the site, if it's still around then.

42. THE CHINESE GOVERNMENT BANS FILMS AND TELEVISION SHOWS THAT CONTAIN TIME TRAVEL.

The government insists that changing historical events is a dangerous subject in fiction. Still, *Avengers: Endgame* earned over $600 million in China, and it's all about time travel, so maybe they apply that law selectively?

43. YODA HAS DIFFERENT NUMBERS OF TOES IN VARIOUS *STAR WARS* FILMS.

In *The Phantom Menace*, he has three, but in *The Empire Strikes Back* and *Return of the Jedi*, and *Revenge of the Sith*, he has four. A special Jedi trick?

44. THE AVERAGE PERSON WILL SPEND ALMOST NINE YEARS OF THEIR LIFE WATCHING TELEVISION OF SOME SORT. THAT'S OVER 78,000 HOURS!

45. THE FILM *HOWARD THE DUCK* WAS A FLOP THAT COST MORE TO MAKE THAN *RETURN OF THE JEDI*.

$37 million vs. $32.5, respectively, to be exact. Both were made by Lucasfilm.

46. TWITTER'S ORIGINAL NAME WAS TWTTR.

Other possibilities were Smssy, Twitch, and Friendstalker. That last one sounds creepy, doesn't it?

47. SAM IN THE MOVIE *CASABLANCA*, COULDN'T ACTUALLY "PLAY IT AGAIN," BECAUSE HE WAS REALLY A DRUMMER AND COULDN'T PLAY THE PIANO.

He played along with the music, imitating a pianist's hand movements offscreen.

48. THE BEATLES' NAME IS NEVER MENTIONED IN THEIR FIRST MOVIE, *A HARD DAY'S NIGHT*.

Though it can be seen on Ringo's drum kit and in a few other places in the film.

• 49 •

THERE ARE TWO SEATS PERMANENTLY BOLTED OPEN AT THE PALACE THEATRE IN LONDON SO THAT GHOSTS CAN SIT IN THEM.

Hey, don't the dead have a right to be entertained the same as the living?

50. IN THE 1970s, GEORGE LUCAS HAD A DOG NAMED "INDIANA."

So now we know where the joke in *Indiana Jones and the Last Crusade* came from! Indiana allegedly also inspired the idea of Chewbacca.

51. SEAN CONNERY WORE A TOUPEE IN EVERY JAMES BOND MOVIE HE WAS IN.

Connery started going bald in the 1960s.

52. MICHAEL MYERS'S WHITE MASK IN THE FIRST *HALLOWEEN* MOVIE IS A PAINTED WILLIAM SHATNER AS CAPTAIN KIRK FACE.

53. GEORGE LUCAS ORIGINALLY WANTED DAVID LYNCH TO DIRECT *RETURN OF THE JEDI*.

Lynch even met with Lucas, but decided it just wasn't for him. Can you imagine how that would've looked?

54. THE BRITISH SHOW *TOP GEAR* IS THE MOST WATCHED TELEVISION SHOW IN THE WORLD.

It's estimated that 350 million people in 170 countries tune in to see it.

55. MARGE SIMPSON WAS ORIGINALLY GOING TO HAVE BUNNY EARS UNDERNEATH HER HAIR.

Creator Matt Groening came up with the idea as a link to his comic strip *Life in Hell*, but abandoned it pretty quickly.

56. *BUFFY THE VAMPIRE SLAYER* WAS THE FIRST TV SHOW TO USE THE WORD "GOOGLE" AS A VERB.

The episode in question was aired in October 2002.

57. HBO ADDED A GUN TO THE *SOPRANOS* LOGOTYPE BECAUSE THE NETWORK WORRIED THAT PEOPLE MIGHT THINK IT WAS A SHOW ABOUT SINGING.

58. EACH HOUR, ABOUT 30,000 SCRABBLE GAMES ARE STARTED AROUND THE WORLD.

59. THE TV SHOW *FRIENDS* HAD SEVERAL DIFFERENT NAMES WHILE IN DEVELOPMENT, INCLUDING "INSOMNIA CAFÉ," "FRIENDS LIKE US," "ACROSS THE HALL," AND "SIX OF ONE."

· 60 ·

SOON AFTER *GILLIGAN'S ISLAND* PREMIERED ON TV IN 1964, THE SHOW BEGAN RECEIVING TELEGRAMS FROM THE COAST GUARD WRITTEN BY VIEWERS ASKING THAT THE CASTAWAYS BE RESCUED.

Reality TV hadn't even been invented yet!

61. TRUE OR FALSE? PEOPLE USUALLY DREAM IN COLOR, BUT MANY WHO GREW UP WATCHING BLACK AND WHITE TELEVISION STILL DREAM IN BLACK AND WHITE.

True. About a quarter of the time, in fact. It seems to have to do with the impressions made on them in childhood.

62. TRUE OR FALSE? BROADWAY IS THE LONGEST STREET IN NEW YORK CITY.

True. It begins in Lower Manhattan and continues north through the Bronx, into Yonkers, and well beyond (as Route 9).

63. TRUE OR FALSE? THERE ARE MORE THAN FORTY BROADWAY THEATERS, BUT ONLY TEN OF THEM ARE ACTUALLY ON BROADWAY.

False. Actually, only four of them are on Broadway: The Winter Garden, The Marquis, The Roundabout, and The Broadway Theatre.

64. TRUE OR FALSE? ON FACEBOOK, YOU CAN CHANGE YOUR LANGUAGE PREFERENCE TO "PIRATE."

Arrrr, it's true!

65. TRUE OR FALSE? ONE BILLION HOURS OF YOUTUBE VIDEOS ARE WATCHED AROUND THE WORLD EVERY DAY.

True. That's a lot of time a lot of people will never get back.

66. TRUE OR FALSE? MORE PEOPLE IN THE WORLD OWN A CELL PHONE THAN A TOOTHBRUSH.

True. It's estimated that there are about 3.7 billion phone owners vs. 3.5 billion toothbrush owners.

67. TRUE OR FALSE? AS OF 2019, IT'S ESTIMATED THAT OVER NINETY-FIVE MILLION PHOTOS ARE UPLOADED TO INSTAGRAM EVERY DAY.

True. That's a whole lot of pictures of babies, pets, and food.

68. TRUE OR FALSE? AS OF MID-2019, MORE THAN 300 HOURS OF VIDEO WERE UPLOADED TO YOUTUBE EVERY MINUTE.

False. It's actually more than 500 hours.

69. TRUE OR FALSE? FACEBOOK IS NOW RATED AS ONE OF THE MAIN CAUSES OF DIVORCE.

True. A 2012 study showed that up to one-third of divorces come from social media disagreements and problems.

• 70 •

TRUE OR FALSE? *THE MATRIX* CODE SYMBOLS COME FROM SUSHI RECIPES.

True. That mysterious green code in the movies is drawn from Japanese script in a sushi cookbook.

DRAGONROLL

TUNASASHIMI

CALIFORNIAROLL

SIDEOFWASABI

AVOCADOROLL

SHRIMPSASHIMI

SPICYTUNAROLL

EELANDAVOCADOROLL

CRABROLL

SALMONSASHIMI

71. TRUE OR FALSE? THE FILMS *ET* AND *POLTERGEIST* CAME FROM THE SAME MOVIE, CALLED *NIGHT SKIES*.

True. *Night Skies* was originally intended to be a darker sequel to Steven Spielberg's *Close Encounters*, but eventually he settled on the more family-friendly *ET*, while some of the scarier elements of *Night Skies* went into *Poltergeist*.

72. TRUE OR FALSE? ABC ONCE PRODUCED A POLICE SHOW THAT WAS A MUSICAL.

True. It was called *Cop Rock*, and it aired for eleven episodes in 1990. The characters would burst into song at various points, and it was about as odd as it sounds.

73. TRUE OR FALSE? FACEBOOK'S POPULATION IS THREE TIMES GREATER THAN THAT OF THE UNITED STATES.

False. It's actually about six times greater. Facebook has over two billion users.

74. TRUE OR FALSE? MICHAEL JACKSON WANTED TO PLAY SPIDER-MAN IN A MOVIE, SO HE ATTEMPTED TO BUY MARVEL COMICS IN THE 1990S TO MAKE IT HAPPEN.

True. It's probably just as well that his plan didn't work out.

75. TRUE OR FALSE? MONOPOLY ACTUALLY HELPED P.O.W.s ESCAPE DURING WORLD WAR II.

True. The Allies were allowed to send modified versions of the game to prisoners in German camps via the Red Cross, but they hid compasses, files, and maps inside, which helped thousands of prisoners to escape.

76. TRUE OR FALSE? THERE ARE MORE WAYS TO ARRANGE A DECK OF PLAYING CARDS THAN THERE ARE ATOMS ON PLANET EARTH.

True. The total amount is an 8 followed by sixty-seven zeroes.

77. TRUE OR FALSE? CHINESE CHECKERS WAS INVENTED BY THE GERMANS, NOT THE CHINESE.

True. The game was invented in Germany in 1892. The name "Chinese Checkers" wasn't introduced until 1928.

78. TRUE OR FALSE? THE LONGEST MONOPOLY GAME EVER PLAYED LASTED FOR FORTY STRAIGHT DAYS.

False. It actually lasted for seventy days, which is 1,680 hours, or about ten weeks!

• 79 •

TRUE OR FALSE? A CONVICTED
MURDERER WAS ONCE GIVEN
A RETRIAL BECAUSE IT WAS
DISCOVERED THAT FOUR OF
THE JURORS HAD CONSULTED
A OUIJA BOARD TO SEE IF HE
WAS GUILTY.

True. They tried to contact the spirit of one
of his alleged victims, who apparently said
he was guilty.

80. TRUE OR FALSE? THE NUMBER OF POSSIBLE CHESS POSITIONS IS ABOUT THE SAME AS THE NUMBER OF STARS IN THE UNIVERSE.

True. The math is a bit complex, but in each case, the number is 10 followed by more than twenty zeros.

81. TRUE OR FALSE? ONE IN FIVE AMERICAN HOUSEHOLDS OWNS A COPY OF SCRABBLE.

False. It's actually about one in three.

82. TRUE OR FALSE? A SUPERMAN REFERENCE OF SOME KIND IS HIDDEN IN EVERY EPISODE OF *SEINFELD*.

False. Jerry Seinfeld's real-life love of Superman did inspire a great many references to the Man of Steel in the show, but contrary to internet rumors there is not one in every single episode.

83. TRUE OR FALSE? THE FIRST AMERICAN TELEVISION STATION STARTED BROADCASTING IN 1938.

False. It was actually ten years earlier, in 1928.

84. TRUE OR FALSE? THE PILOT FOR THE TV SHOW *LOST* WAS SO EXPENSIVE THAT THE CHAIRMAN OF ABC WAS FIRED FOR GOING AHEAD WITH IT.

True. Lloyd Braun was enthusiastic about the show, but his superiors weren't happy with him, because they thought it was way too expensive ($13 million for the pilot episode!). But the show went on to become a massive hit, and Braun had the last laugh.

85. TRUE OR FALSE? THE FILM *TOY STORY 2* WAS ALMOST ACCIDENTALLY DELETED.

True. Someone at Pixar mistakenly ran a command to delete everything from a particular system. Also, the backup files had failed to work properly. Thankfully, one employee was working from home and had most of the missing files on her own computer, so the film was saved.

Food

PECULIAR FOOD AND DRINK FACTS

We all have our favorite foods. We need food to live, but also to truly enjoy life. If we only had one thing to eat all the time, our lives would get very boring, very fast. Thankfully, there is an almost infinite variety of foods to choose from, and there is always something new and, frankly, weird for you to try if you're brave enough. And foods themselves offer us no shortage of the strange and unlikely, from their biology to their cultivation to how they're made and where they come from. Here for your dining pleasure is a smorgasbord of freaky food facts.

1. WHEN SEALED, HONEY DOESN'T GO BAD.

Due to its chemical composition, it can stay edible for thousands
of years, as long as the lid is sealed tight to prevent moisture
from getting in.

2. THE ALMOND ISN'T A NUT AND IS RELATED TO THE PEACH.

Peach pits even look a bit like almonds, but don't eat them.
They are bitter and contain cyanide.

3. EGGPLANTS ARE BERRIES.

A berry is a fruit without a stone that develops from a flower
with one ovary. Eggplant ("aubergine" in many European
countries) meets all those conditions. Maybe we should call it the
"eggberry" instead?

• 4 •

A LOT OF COMMERCIAL ICE CREAMS HAVE SEAWEED IN THEM.

Known as agar, it's a thickening agent used in all sorts of food, but don't worry, it won't make your cookie dough ice cream taste like low tide.

5. POTATOES HAVE MORE CHROMOSOMES THAN HUMANS.

They have forty-eight, while we have forty-six. But just because spuds have more chromosomes doesn't mean they are a higher form of life; it's just a quirk of evolution. Lots of animals have more chromosomes than humans, including the carp, which has 104.

6. IF YOU PUT TONIC WATER UNDER BLACK LIGHT IT SHINES BRIGHT BLUE.

Tonic water contains quinine, which has a chemical that is fluorescent under ultraviolet light. That combination could make for some interesting mixed drinks.

7. RANCH DRESSING CONTAINS TITANIUM DIOXIDE, WHICH IS ALSO USED IN SUNSCREEN TO GIVE IT ITS WHITE COLOR.

8. CASU MARZU IS A TRADITIONAL CHEESE FROM SARDINIA THAT CONTAINS LIVE MAGGOTS.

The idea is that they digest the cheese fat, which is what makes it very soft and spreadable. But the little creatures can jump up to six inches, so one has to eat the cheese with a hand over it. As you might imagine, it's been outlawed by the European Union for health reasons. That's what the maggot cheese black market is for.

9. IN 2008, A FROSTED FLAKE SHAPED LIKE ILLINOIS SOLD ON EBAY FOR $1,350.

The buyer wanted to add it to a traveling museum of Americana. People really will buy anything on the internet!

10. CHEESE IS THE MOST WIDELY SHOPLIFTED FOOD IN THE WORLD.

It's small, easy to conceal, and in high demand. But probably not the Sardinian maggot cheese mentioned on the previous page.

11. NO ONE IS QUITE SURE WHERE FRENCH FRIES WERE INVENTED.

Belgium is often listed as the birthplace of the fry, but the era pointed to (the late 1600s) is off, since the region didn't seem to have the potato until decades later. Also, fat was expensive and deep frying would have been out of the question. The French had something like them in the later eighteenth century, sold by food peddlers with carts. But who created them first? We may never know.

12. POPCORN ORIGINALLY WASN'T A FAVORITE MOVIE SNACK.

Movie theaters actually hated it. They wanted to be seen as "theaters," and silent films required a literate audience, so no "upscale" theater would allow food in the seats. With the advent of talkies, however, movies became popular entertainment for everyone, and attitudes changed.

• 13 •

IN THE LATER MIDDLE AGES, A POPULAR FOOD DISH AMONG THE NOBILITY WAS KNOWN AS "GARBAGE."

It was mixture of chicken heads, feet, and organs in a stew with expensive spices.

14. THERE ARE ABOUT 7,500 VARIETIES OF APPLES GROWN ALL OVER THE WORLD.

If you ate a new one every day it would take you more than twenty years to try them all.

15. TARANTULA BRANDY IS A POPULAR DRINK IN CAMBODIA.

It's exactly what you think it is, only worse. The tarantulas are usually tossed live into the drink. Deep fried tarantulas are also popular there as a snack.

16. AMERICANS EAT ENOUGH HAMBURGERS EACH YEAR THAT THE BURGERS WOULD STRETCH AROUND THE EARTH ABOUT THIRTY-TWO TIMES.

Fifty billion burgers, in fact!

17. A POPULAR RECIPE IN ANCIENT ROME WAS BRAINS AND BACON.

Pig or calf brains, to be precise. It often also had hard-boiled eggs and chicken giblets.

18. IN KENTUCKY, IT'S ILLEGAL TO CARRY AN ICE CREAM CONE IN YOUR BACK POCKET.

It's an old law in several states that was created to prevent horse theft. Thieves would put the cone in their back pockets to lure away horses, apparently. It's still on the books, but not actually enforced today, by the way.

19. IN NEW ENGLAND IN THE EIGHTEENTH AND NINETEENTH CENTURIES, LOBSTERS WERE CONSIDERED LITTLE BETTER THAN RATS, AND WERE ONLY FED TO PRISONERS AND THE POOR.

The bottom feeders only started to become popular in the 1880s, with inlanders who didn't know they were considered trash food. And thus a delicacy was born!

20. YOU CAN BUY GRILLED CHICKEN BUTTHOLES ON A STICK IN TAIPEI, TAIWAN.

The question is... why?

21. THE PUFFERFISH CONTAINS A TOXIN 1,200 TIMES DEADLIER THAN CYANIDE, BUT PEOPLE STILL EAT IT.

In Japan, where it is a delicacy, it has to be prepared by a highly trained chef, or it would easily kill the person eating it. But people still order it at select restaurants, and occasionally die.

• 22 •

THE SOURTOE COCKTAIL IS A MUMMIFIED TOE IN AN ALCOHOLIC DRINK.

It's served by the Sourtoe Cocktail Club in Dawson City, Yukon, Canada. To join the club, you must drink the cocktail with the toe in it. Several toes have been donated for use over the years, because sometimes people have accidentally (and one time, intentionally) swallowed them!

23. "PUMPERNICKEL" MEANS "DEVIL'S FART."

The New High German word *pumpern* means "flatulent," while *Nickel* refers to a goblin or "Old Nick," a slang term for the Devil. The word may be older than the bread and meant as an insult to a flatulent person.

24. WATERMELON IS THE OFFICIAL VEGETABLE OF OKLAHOMA.

Yes, the vegetable. The official state fruit is the strawberry.

25. FROM THE RENAISSANCE TO THE NINETEENTH CENTURY, SOME DOCTORS PRESCRIBED EATING PARTS OF CORPSES AND MUMMIES FOR HEALTH.

The dried bits were crumbled into things like chocolate and alcohol and given to treat headaches, bleeding, and other ailments.

26. IT'S POSSIBLE TO MAKE DIAMONDS OUT OF PEANUT BUTTER.

Peanut butter contains a lot of carbon, the principle component of a diamond. Add enough pressure and heat and you'll get little fragments of diamond. You probably won't be making necklaces out of them anytime soon, though.

27. IN MARION, OREGON, MINISTERS ARE NOT ALLOWED TO EAT GARLIC OR ONIONS BEFORE DELIVERING THEIR SERMONS.

It's easy to understand why, really.

28. EATING JUNK FOOD CHANGES BRAIN ACTIVITY IN A WAY SIMILAR TO ADDICTIVE DRUGS.

Studies have shown that foods high in sugar and fat trigger dopamine in the brain, a "pleasure" hormone. Too much of these foods leads to cravings and addiction. MRI scans have shown that the same areas of the brain light up with junk foods as with certain drugs.

29. IN SOUTH DAKOTA, IT'S ILLEGAL TO LIE DOWN AND FALL ASLEEP IN A CHEESE FACTORY.

30. IN SOUTH KOREA, PEOPLE WATCH SHOWS OF OTHER PEOPLE EATING.

Called a *mukbang*, it is a live internet broadcast during which the host eats various foods and interacts with the audience. Some viewers even pay for the privilege, depending on the show. One reason given for these shows' popularity is that the vicarious act of watching others eating is similar to watching cooking shows. Further, the host usually chats with viewers, so there is audience participation.

• 31 •

PISTACHIOS CAN BE FLAMMABLE, AND EVEN EXPLODE.

This is due to their high fat and low water content. Even after they've been harvested they have to be stored carefully. Ships transporting them have special regulations to follow so they don't blow up on board.

32. FRIED SCORPIONS ON A STICK ARE EATEN AS A LUXURY SNACK IN CHINA.

The flavor seems to take the sting out of the high price. Get it? The "sting"?

33. POPE ADRIAN IV (CA. 1100-159) WAS SAID TO HAVE DIED BY CHOKING ON A FLY THAT HAD LANDED IN HIS WINE.

34. SPAM IS SHORT FOR "SPICED HAM."

It makes sense, if you think about it.

35. WHEN MCDONALD'S OPENED ITS FIRST RESTAURANT IN KUWAIT IN 1994, THE LINE OF CARS WAITING FOR THE DRIVE THROUGH WAS SEVEN MILES LONG.

It's estimated that there were about 15,000 people in the line.

36. A SINGLE PIECE OF SPAGHETTI IS TECHNICALLY A "SPAGHETTO."

37. PEANUTS ARE AN INGREDIENT IN DYNAMITE.

Peanut oil can produce glycerol, which is used to make nitroglycerine, an explosive component in dynamite. Think about that when you bite into your next PB&J!

38. IN NEBRASKA, IT'S AGAINST THE LAW FOR BAR OWNERS TO SELL BEER UNLESS THEY ARE ALSO COOKING A KETTLE OF SOUP AT THE SAME TIME.

39. EACH BANANA YOU EAT IS A CLONE.

Cavendish bananas account for over 95% of the world's banana supply, and they are all genetically identical. They are sterile and have to be reproduced by cloning, through cuttings and tissue culturing.

40. WITHOUT FLIES CHOCOLATE WOULDN'T EXIST.

The flies, known as biting midges, are a scourge of campers and outdoor people. Sometimes known as chocolate midges or "No See Ums," these little creatures are the only species that pollinates the cacao tree. No midges, no chocolate!

41. THE APPLES YOU BUY IN THE SUPERMARKET CAN BE ALMOST A YEAR OLD.

They remain fresh because they were in cold storage, where they can last for over ten months. Sometimes they are also treated with a gaseous compound called 1-methylcyclopropene, which is considered a safe additive to stop them from rotting.

• 42 •

AN ORANGE WITH ITS PEEL INTACT FLOATS IN WATER, BUT A PEELED ORANGE SINKS.

This has to do with the structure of the outer peel, which is porous and filled with little air pockets. These cause the orange to be less dense than water, so it floats. Take the peel away, and the inside is denser, so it sinks. It's like removing a life jacket.

43. CRANBERRIES WILL BOUNCE LIKE RUBBER BALLS WHEN RIPE.

This is due to a small air pocket inside. Overripe cranberries will just land with a thud. In fact, this is a good way to test for ripeness.

44. CALIFORNIA'S HASS AVOCADOS CAN ALL BE TRACED BACK TO A TREE PLANTED IN 1926.

Postman Rudolph Hass planted some avocado seeds on his property in La Habra Heights (now swallowed up by Los Angeles). One produced a fruit that tasted better than the others, and the Hass avocado was born from that.

45. REGULAR CORN COBS ALWAYS HAVE AN EVEN NUMBER OF ROWS, QUITE OFTEN SIXTEEN.

This has to do with the way the corn flowers grow in double rows in the early stages of the corn ear's development.

46. COCA-COLA ONCE TRIED TO REPLACE COFFEE AS THE FAVORITE MORNING DRINK.

The idea was that the sugary and caffeinated soda was easier to drink than having to prepare coffee. "Coke in the Morning" was a trial promotion in 1988 to unseat coffee as the breakfast king. It didn't work.

47. SNICKERS ARE NAMED AFTER A HORSE.

In 1930, Frank Mars introduced the chocolate bar, naming it after his family's favorite horse.

48. IN NEWARK, NEW JERSEY, IT'S AGAINST THE LAW TO SELL ICE CREAM AFTER 6:00 PM, UNLESS THE CUSTOMER PRODUCES A NOTE FROM HIS DOCTOR.

49. ORANGES CAN BE GREEN AND FULLY RIPE.

The green just means that they are full of chlorophyll. When they turn orange in color, it's an indication that the chlorophyll has faded. In fact, orange-colored oranges are closer to being over-ripe and decaying.

50. ENGLISH MUFFINS AREN'T MUFFINS. OR ENGLISH.

They were indeed invented by a British man, Samuel Bath Thomas. But he was an ex-pat living in New York in the 1880s. He fashioned them after the English crumpet. In 1894, someone coined the term "English muffin" and it stuck.

• 51 •

CELLULOSE GUM, THE
INGREDIENT THAT GIVES
THE FILLING IN TWINKIES
A SMOOTH AND CREAMY
FEEL, IS ALSO FOUND
IN ROCKET FUEL.

52. TWINKIES ORIGINALLY HAD A BANANA-FLAVORED FILLING, BUT HAD TO CHANGE TO VANILLA WHEN WORLD WAR II DISRUPTED THE BANANA TRADE.

It was finally reintroduced permanently in 2005.

53. FOOD PHOTOGRAPHERS SOMETIMES USE MASHED POTATOES INSTEAD OF ACTUAL ICE CREAM IN ICE CREAM PHOTOS.

They've also been known to use frosting and even Play Doh. Yum!

54. IN GAINESVILLE, GEORGIA, IT'S AGAINST THE LAW TO EAT FRIED CHICKEN WITH ANYTHING BUT YOUR HANDS.

It was a joke law that was passed in 1961 for the city to gain some publicity as a poultry producer, but it's still on the books.

55. ABOUT 99% OF ALL THE WASABI SOLD IN THE UNITED STATES IS FAKE.

It's a mixture of horseradish, hot mustard, and green dye. So, no matter how much sushi you've eaten, if you've eaten it in America you've probably never tasted real wasabi. Even in Japan, about 95% of "wasabi" is fake, because the real stuff is hard to grow and very expensive.

56. YOU CAN HEAR RHUBARB GROW.

It's often left in fields for two years, where it gathers energy from the sun. It is then taken into a darkened shed and the stored energy makes the stalks grow bigger and sweeter. During this time, you can hear the buds opening. They make creaking and cracking sounds as they grow rapidly.

57. FOOD IS ALLOWED TO CONTAIN CERTAIN TRACE AMOUNTS OF INSECTS, HAIR, AND POOP.

In the United States, the FDA sets safe levels for various foreign substances: coffee beans can have 10 milligrams of animal poop per pound, peanut butter can have about 30 insect fragments for every 100 grams, canned tomatoes can have up to two maggots in a 16-ounce can, while frozen spinach can contain as many as 50 aphids or mites. There are a lot more examples, but we'll stop there, or you'll never eat again!

58. PUMPKINS ARE BERRIES.

Like eggplants, and for the same reasons. Kind of mind-blowing, isn't it?

59. A FAVORITE DESSERT KILLED KING ADOLF FREDERICK OF SWEDEN IN 1771.

The treat in question was *hetvägg*, a sweet roll with whipped cream, and he downed fourteen servings of it, after a dinner of lobster, caviar, and Champagne, among other things, so it's not that surprising.

• 60 •

ARTIFICIAL VANILLA FLAVOR CONTAINS A SUBSTANCE CALLED CASTOREUM, WHICH COMES FROM A GLAND IN A BEAVER'S BUTT.

Beavers use it to mark their territory. The FDA considers it "generally safe," and a "natural flavoring." Apparently, it smells like vanilla, too.

61. TRUE OR FALSE? PEARLS FLOAT IN VINEGAR.

False. They actually dissolve, and it can happen in as little as ten minutes. So watch your pearls around the salad!

62. TRUE OR FALSE? PEZ CANDIES WERE FIRST MARKETED AS AN ANTI-SMOKING DEVICE.

True. Introduced in the late 1920s, they were mint-flavored and designed to help smokers take their minds off of cigarettes.

63. TRUE OR FALSE? ARACHIBUTYROPHOBIA IS THE FEAR OF ACCIDENTALLY EATING A SPIDER.

False. It's the fear of getting peanut butter stuck to the top of your mouth.

64. TRUE OR FALSE? HAWAIIAN PIZZA WAS INVENTED IN BRAZIL.

False. It was invented in Canada. Greek-Canadian cook and restaurant owner Sam Panopoulos claimed to have invented the controversial combination (pizza topped with pineapple and ham) in Ontario in 1962. The idea of calling it "Hawaiian" came from the name on the canned pineapple he used in those early days.

65. TRUE OR FALSE? THE AZTECS USED CHOCOLATE AS CURRENCY.

True. They associated it with the god Quetzacoatl, who they believed had given it to humanity as a gift. Chocolate was used for tribute, taxes, and even to buy boats.

66. TRUE OR FALSE? GERMAN CHOCOLATE CAKE COMES FROM GERMANY.

False. It was created based on chocolate developed by Samuel German for Baker's Chocolate Company, in the United States. A recipe titled "German's Chocolate Cake" appeared in 1957, but later the name was changed to "German Chocolate Cake."

67. TRUE OR FALSE? EACH PINEAPPLE PLANT ONLY PRODUCES THREE PINEAPPLES IN ITS LIFETIME.

False. Each plant actually only produces one.

68. TRUE OR FALSE? THE VICTORIANS HAD A RECIPE FOR A TOAST SANDWICH, WHICH IS EXACTLY WHAT IT SOUNDS LIKE.

True. A piece of toasted bread was put between two pieces of untoasted bread, with a little salt and pepper added for taste. It was thought to be a good mild food for invalids and the ill.

· 69 ·

TRUE OR FALSE? IN CHICAGO, IT'S ILLEGAL TO FISH WHILE WEARING YOUR PAJAMAS.

True. Just keep that in mind when visiting the Windy City.

70. TRUE OR FALSE? FIGS CONTAIN DEAD WASPS.

True, sort of. A fig is not a fruit, it's an inverted flower, and needs to be pollinated by the fig wasp. These wasps are hatched inside figs, and the females crawl out, carrying pollen with them to take to another fig. The males remain inside and die, but the fig digests and absorbs them so there's nothing left of them by the time you eat one. Any crunch still left inside a fig is just seeds.

71. TRUE OR FALSE? WHITE CHOCOLATE IS ACTUALLY REAL CHOCOLATE.

False. White chocolate does have cocoa butter, but doesn't have chocolate solids, which is what defines chocolate as chocolate.

72. TRUE OR FALSE? IN ANCIENT ROME, THE GROOM SEALED HIS MARRIAGE BY SMASHING A BARLEY CAKE OVER HIS BRIDE'S HEAD.

True. It was a bit of a crumbly start to the marriage.

73. TRUE OR FALSE? THE RED FOOD-COLORING CARMINE—USED IN ALL KINDS OF CANDIES, FOODS, COSMETICS, AND PAINT—IS MADE FROM COCHINEAL BUGS.

True. When dried and crushed, they produce a red dye.

74. TRUE OR FALSE? THE STICKERS ON GROCERY STORE FRUIT ARE EDIBLE.

True. But you probably shouldn't make a habit of eating them.

75. TRUE OR FALSE? CARROTS WERE ORIGINALLY PURPLE OR WHITE.

True. That's how they looked when they originated in Afghanistan, and later in Europe. It was the Dutch in the seventeenth century that bred the orange carrots we know and love today.

76. TRUE OR FALSE? IN ANCIENT GREECE, THROWING AN APPLE AT SOMEONE WAS A WAY TO PROPOSE MARRIAGE.

False. This misconception sometimes shows up on the internet. Tossing an apple might be seen as an act of seduction, since apples were associated with the goddess Aphrodite, but marriages were not planned that way.

77. TRUE OR FALSE? IN FAIRBANKS, ALASKA, IT'S AGAINST THE LAW TO GIVE AN ALCOHOLIC BEVERAGE TO A MOOSE.

True. But then, why would you do this to begin with?

• 78 •

TRUE OR FALSE?
POTATOES ABSORB AND
REFLECT WI-FI SIGNALS.

True. Researchers at Boeing discovered that, due to their water content and chemical composition, spuds act on radio signals not unlike humans do.

79. TRUE OR FALSE? CELERY HAS NEGATIVE CALORIES.

False. While it's true that a lot of the caloric content of celery is in cellulose, which is a fiber that humans can't digest, it still provides about six calories per stalk and we only need half a calorie of energy (or less) to digest it.

80. TRUE OR FALSE? NUTMEG CAN CAUSE HALLUCINATIONS AND SEIZURES.

True. It contains a substance called myristicin that in larger amounts affects the sympathetic nervous system. You'd need to ingest a lot, though, so the nutmeg in your pumpkin pie and eggnog is just fine.

81. TRUE OR FALSE? COCA-COLA ORIGINALLY CONTAINED COCAINE.

True. The drink was originally sold as a medicine. The "Coca" part of the name referred to the plant from which cocaine is derived. The "Cola" was from the kola nut. Both were ingredients. The soda still had trace amounts of cocaine in it as late as 1929.

82. TRUE OR FALSE? COCONUT WATER CAN BE USED AS A SUBSTITUTE FOR HUMAN BLOOD.

False. This misconception has been going around the internet for a while, but it's not the same as plasma, and shouldn't be used in place of it. Coconut water is useful for rehydration, though.

83. TRUE OR FALSE? ADDING OIL TO BOILING WATER KEEPS PASTA FROM STICKING.

False. Oil has no real affect. Most of it floats on the top of the water. Stirring the pasta regularly works better.

84. TRUE OR FALSE? SALTED WATER BOILS MORE QUICKLY.

False. Salt actually increases the boiling point of water to 216°F instead of the regular 212°F.

85. TRUE OR FALSE? IN OKLAHOMA, IT'S ILLEGAL TO TAKE A BITE OF SOMEONE ELSE'S HAMBURGER.

False. Many states do have weird, outdated laws, but this one seems to be an urban legend.

Odds and Ends

MISCELLANEOUS ODDITIES

There is no shortage of strange facts in the world (and beyond), and sometimes it's fun just to put a whole pile of them together in one place and see what happens. So here's a blend of what's come before, plus plenty of odds and ends that don't quite fit in elsewhere. This assortment of the uncommon is the perfect way to wrap things up, demonstrating how the world we live in is weird and wonderful, indeed.

1. MARTIAN SUNSETS ARE BLUE.

This is because the dust in the Martian atmosphere scatters the red light, making the sky look reddish. But at sunset, the light from the sun must travel farther, so it scatters more, leaving the blueish color as the one most visible. The exact opposite happens on Earth, which is why our sunsets appear pink, orange, and red.

2. THE MAJORITY OF YOUR BRAIN IS MADE UP OF FAT.

About 60%, in fact. So calling someone a "fathead" isn't really much of an insult.

3. RUSSIA'S SURFACE AREA IS ONLY SLIGHTLY SMALLER THAN THE SURFACE AREA OF PLUTO.

Russia's total surface area is listed as 17,125,191 square kilometers, while Pluto's has been corrected by the recent New Horizon mission to be 17,646,012 square kilometers. So, either Russia is really big, or Pluto is pretty small, depending on how you look at it.

4. A MILLION SECONDS IS ABOUT ELEVEN DAYS, WHILE A BILLION SECONDS IS JUST UNDER THIRTY-TWO YEARS.

• 5 •

A DUEL BETWEEN THREE PEOPLE IS TECHNICALLY KNOWN AS A "TRUEL."

Three-way duels have been described since at least the nineteenth century, but the word itself was introduced in the 1960s, in books about game theory and gambling.

6. QWERTY KEYBOARDS WERE NOT ORIGINALLY INTENDED TO SLOW DOWN TYPING SPEED.

This is a popular belief, based on the idea that early typewriters would jam if typists worked too quickly, but it's not true. The layout of the letter order evolved over time and came mainly from telegraph users transcribing Morse code. A standard alphabetical arrangement proved to be inefficient for them, whereas the QWERTY system was more workable.

7. IF YOU COULD FOLD A PIECE OF PAPER FORTY-TWO TIMES, IT WOULD BE THICK ENOUGH TO REACH THE MOON.

If you could fold it 103 times, it would be larger than the observable universe. This bizarre fact is based on the act of doubling the thickness with each fold. The problem is, our sheets of paper are far too small to do it. You'd need a piece of paper about 107,000 light years across, which is a bit larger than the Milky Way Galaxy.

8. A MEGA-COLONY OF ANTS LIVES ALL OVER THE WORLD.

There is a colony of Argentine ants along the Mediterranean that is over 3,700 miles along, another over 500 miles long in California, and others in Japan. The thing is, when ants from these separate colonies are put together, they are friendly and interact with each other, indicating that they are related and come from the same original colony.

9. MEN ARE 23% MORE LIKELY TO BE LEFT-HANDED THAN WOMEN.

Various theories have been put forward as to why, but we're still not sure of the reason.

10. THERE ARE ABOUT 60,000 MILES OF BLOOD VESSELS IN A SINGLE HUMAN BODY.

If they were all laid out end-to-end, of course. Some estimates say it's even more.

11. PRESIDENT ULYSSES S. GRANT WAS ARRESTED FOR SPEEDING ON A HORSE.

There are various versions of the story, but policeman William H. West saw President Grant going too fast on the streets of Washington, D.C., and issued him a warning. Grant did the same thing the next day, and West arrested him. Grant had to put up $20 as collateral, but never showed up for his trial.

12. A FAMILY OF PEOPLE WITH BLUE-COLORED SKIN LIVED IN KENTUCKY FOR SEVERAL GENERATIONS.

The Fugates family carried a genetic trait that caused a disease called methemoglobinemia, in which the hemoglobin can't carry oxygen. One of the symptoms can be blue skin. The last known family member to show this trait was born in 1975.

• 13 •

ANT QUEENS CAN LIVE FOR UP TO THIRTY YEARS.

Unfortunately, worker ants aren't blessed with such longevity, with life spans of only up to three years. And males have it even worse, often living only a few weeks. It's good to be the queen!

14. MOST LAUGHTER ISN'T JUST BECAUSE SOMETHING IS FUNNY.

Studies have shown that we are thirty times more likely to laugh when we are with other people, especially friends and family. Laughter is a form of communication and bonding, and we often laugh at things that others say, even when they aren't funny.

15. IN SWITZERLAND, IT'S ILLEGAL FOR PEOPLE TO OWN JUST ONE GUINEA PIG.

Guinea pigs are herd animals, and a study determined that it was cruel for them to live alone. What if you have two and one dies? Well, there are places where you can rent guinea pigs for companionship.

16. CHAINSAWS WERE INVENTED TO AID CHILDBIRTH.

This seems utterly horrifying, but a form of hand-operated chainsaw was invented in the late eighteenth century to assist difficult childbirths. It could cut through cartilage and even bone to help free a baby that was stuck. The intention was to save both the baby and the mother, and it often worked. It was used for other kinds of surgeries during the nineteenth century. Don't worry, chainsaws for wood came much later and weren't used on people, except in horror movies.

17. FOR OVER A HUNDRED YEARS, MAPS SHOWED A SMALL ISLAND THAT DOESN'T ACTUALLY EXIST.

Named Sandy Island, it was first recorded in 1876 as being in the South Pacific, east of Australia. It was noted on various maps for over a century, until 1979, when some scientists sailed to the location and found nothing there. It still showed up on maps, including Google's, until 2012. It seems the original ship's crew either mis-located another island, or maybe saw an overturned barge and mistook it for a small land mass.

18. IN PROVIDENCE, RHODE ISLAND, IT'S AGAINST THE LAW TO SELL BOTH TOOTHPASTE AND A TOOTHBRUSH TO THE SAME CUSTOMER ON A SUNDAY.

19. WOMBAT POOP IS SHAPED LIKE CUBES.

It seems to have something to do with the dry climate they live in and the shape of their intestines, but it's still being studied. "What do you do for a living? I study wombat poop!"

20. LONDON RENTS TWO PIECES OF LAND FROM THE CROWN FOR A KNIFE, AN AX, HORSESHOES, AND NAILS.

This strange price has a name: the Ceremony of Quit Rents. It dates to the early thirteenth century. No one knows where the land is any more. One piece is in London, the other is in Shropshire, on the border with Wales. Each year in October (sometimes November), the city pays the monarchy a knife, an ax, six horseshoes, and sixty-one nails.

A DUCK, A SHEEP, AND A ROOSTER WERE THE FIRST PASSENGERS IN A EUROPEAN HOT AIR BALLOON.

Brothers Joseph-Michel and Jacques-Étienne Montgolfier demonstrated their version of a hot air balloon at Versailles in September 1783. King Louis XVI suggested sending up some convicted criminals, but the brothers opted for farm animals instead. The balloon stayed aloft for several minutes before landing in a forest a few miles away. The animals were unharmed, and the flight was deemed a success.

• 22 •

IN TOKYO, YOU CAN BUY A WIG FOR YOUR DOG.

They are sold in vending machines and come in all sorts of styles. Seriously.

23. MAINE IS THE ONLY STATE WITH A ONE-SYLLABLE NAME.

Look it up.

24. THE *APOLLO 11* ASTRONAUTS HAD TO GO THROUGH CUSTOMS WHEN THEY RETURNED FROM THE MOON.

They had to declare their moon rocks and other lunar material and sign a form, just like the rest of us do when entering any foreign country.

25. THE DINOSAURS LIVED ON EARTH FOR 150 MILLION YEARS; HUMANS HAVE BEEN HERE FOR 0.13% OF THAT TIME.

We've been around for about 200,000 years, a mere 1/750th of the time that the dinosaurs lived!

26. IF YOU WERE TO SPELL OUT NUMBERS IN ENGLISH, YOU WOULD HAVE TO GO TO ONE THOUSAND UNTIL YOU'D USE THE LETTER "A."

27. HIPPOPOTOMONSTROSESQUIPPEDALIOPHOBIA IS THE FEAR OF LONG WORDS.

28. A BITE FROM THE LONE STAR TICK CAN MAKE YOU ALLERGIC TO MEAT.

It can pass on a condition known as Alpha-gal syndrome, symptoms of which can include upset stomach, indigestion, shortness of breath, coughing, dizziness, vomiting, and various other unpleasant reactions after eating meat.

29. THE COMPUTER MOUSE WAS ONCE CALLED A TURTLE.

The name was changed because the cord connecting it to a computer looked like a mouse's tail. The second name stuck and we still use it, even with the more common cordless versions we have now.

30. BLOOD FALLS IN ANTARCTICA REGULARLY POURS OUT RED LIQUID FROM TAYLOR GLACIER, WHICH MAKES IT LOOK LIKE THE ICE IS BLEEDING.

The water in the lake underneath contains an iron-rich brine that gives it a macabre, red color as it flows out.

31. ONE MAN HAD A BOUT OF HICCUPS THAT LASTED FOR SIXTY-EIGHT YEARS.

Charles Osborne (1894-1991) started his long-term bout of hiccups in 1922, after a slight brain injury kept it from inhibiting his hiccup response. They stopped the year before he died, so he got some peace at last before resting in peace.

• 32 •

BABE RUTH WAS SAID TO HAVE PUT A CABBAGE LEAF UNDER HIS CAP WHEN PLAYING BASEBALL, TO KEEP HIS HEAD COOL.

Recently, the practice has been banned in South Korean baseball as a "foreign substance," unless the player has a doctor's note explaining why it's needed.

33. COWS KILL MORE PEOPLE EACH YEAR THAN SHARKS DO.

Sharks kill approximately four people each year, while cows are responsible for twenty-two annual deaths on average.

34. JOUSTING IS THE STATE SPORT OF MARYLAND.

It was named so in 1962.

35. CROWS REMEMBER FACES FOR YEARS.

Studies have shown that if a crow has a negative association with a face or views it as threatening, it can remember that face years after the experience and will taunt or even dive-bomb the person long after the unpleasant event.

36. NINE-BANDED ARMADILLOS ALWAYS GIVE BIRTH TO IDENTICAL QUADRUPLETS.

Its single egg splits into four identical embryos that will always be the same sex.

37. "LA MARCHA REAL," THE SPANISH NATIONAL ANTHEM, HAS NO WORDS.

38. WHEN QUEEN ELIZABETH VISITED THE GAME OF THRONES SET IN NORTHERN IRELAND, SHE DIDN'T SIT ON THE IRON THRONE BECAUSE A BRITISH MONARCH IS NOT ALLOWED TO SIT ON A FOREIGN THRONE.

Not even a fictional one, apparently.

39. SAUDI ARABIA IMPORTS CAMELS FROM AUSTRALIA.

Saudi Arabian camels are mainly bred for racing and riding, while the imported camels are meant for the dinner table.

40. THE FIRST AMERICAN RACING CAR IN 1895 REACHED A SPEED OF ABOUT 7 MPH.

Known as the *Chicago Times-Herald* Race, it featured six vehicles, and the course was fifty-four miles long. The winner took a little over ten hours to complete the race. Only one other car also crossed the finish line.

41. A QUEEN TERMITE CAN LIVE UP TO FIFTY YEARS.

That's a lot of time to oversee the wood eating.

42. KENTUCKY CURRENTLY HAS MORE BOURBON BARRELS THAN PEOPLE.

It has over nine million barrels of spirits aging away, and about half that number of humans.

• 43 •

IN 1992, 28,000 RUBBER DUCK BATH TOYS WERE LOST AT SEA ON THE WAY FROM HONG KONG TO THE UNITED STATES.

They are still being found on shores around the word. Places as far-flung as Alaska, Australia, and Scotland have reported rubber ducks washing up on beaches.

44. THE WORDS ANIMAL, CITIZEN, FIFTH, DANGEROUS, WOLF, ORANGE, DELICIOUS AND BULB (AMONG OTHERS) HAVE NO WORDS IN ENGLISH THAT RHYME WITH THEM.

45. DOLLY PARTON ONCE ENTERED A DOLLY PARTON LOOK-ALIKE CONTEST... AND LOST.

It was in Los Angeles, and the event was a drag queen celebrity look-alike competition. She entered for fun and kept her identity secret, and the judges decided that someone else did her better than she did!

46. THE HUMAN LIVER CAN REGROW ITSELF IN SEVERAL WEEKS.

The liver is the only organ that can regenerate. Even if more than 50% of it is damaged it will repair itself in a month or less. It can completely regrow even if 75% is lost.

47. THERE'S A FENCE IN AUSTRALIA THAT'S LONGER THAN THE DISTANCE BETWEEN MIAMI AND SEATTLE.

It's called the Dingo Fence and stretches from south-central to eastern Australia to keep dingoes away from sheep flocks and other potential prey. It's 3,488 miles long, while the distance between Miami and Seattle is just over 3,300 miles.

48. A MANTIS SHRIMP CAN PACK A PUNCH SO FAST THAT IT BOILS THE WATER AROUND IT.

Sort of. Its claw accelerates at a remarkable speed to break the shells of clams and other hard-shelled creatures. In doing so, it vaporizes the water around it, producing bubbles that then collapse in a process known as cavitation. These bubbles can actually damage ship propellers and other underwater constructions.

49. APPROXIMATELY 50% OF ALL THE GOLD EVER MINED BY HUMANS HAS BEEN MINED SINCE 1967.

There's a lot more still in the earth, but much of it is unrecoverable since it is found deep in the ocean and the planet's core.

50. THE SCENT OF CHOCOLATE MAKES PEOPLE WANT TO BUY ROMANCE NOVELS.

A study in Belgium showed that people were 40% more likely to buy romance novels or cookbooks if the smell of chocolate was in the air, and 22% more likely to buy books in general. Maybe this is why so many bookstores now have cafes?

51. AS MANY AS 40,000 AMERICANS ARE INJURED BY TOILETS EACH YEAR.

This is due to everything from cracked seats and too much straining to spider and other critter bites.

52. THERE MAY BE AS MANY AS 2,000 SERIAL KILLERS IN THE UNITED STATES RIGHT NOW.

Researcher Thomas Hargrove came to that conclusion after analyzing FBI and other data. There's a thought that'll keep you awake at night.

53. THE HASKELL OPERA HOUSE IS LOCATED BOTH IN CANADA AND THE UNITED STATES.

Its stage is in Quebec, while a good number of the seats are in Vermont.

54. QUEEN ELIZABETH II'S DAIRY COWS SLEEP ON WATERBEDS.

At the royal farm at Windsor Great Park, more than 160 dairy cows get special treatment, including water-filled pillows to sleep and lounge on. Not a bad life!

55. SINGAPORE BANS THE SALE OF CHEWING GUM.

This was in response to widespread vandalism; used gum was littering streets and buildings, and even train doors were being stuck together. The ban is still in place, though certain types of gum (nicotine and dental health) are now permitted.

56. SCIENTISTS MANAGED TO SLOW DOWN THE SPEED OF LIGHT TO 38 MPH.

These researchers shot a laser through very cold sodium atoms and reduced its speed that far down. To clarify, light always travels at the same speed, but by putting this obstacle in the way the experiment was able to force the photon to interact with other particles, thus delaying its arrival.

57. FRANCE EXECUTED A MAN BY GUILLOTINE IN THE SAME YEAR THAT THE FIRST *STAR WARS* MOVIE CAME OUT.

Convicted murderer Hamida Djandoubi was executed in February 1977, the last to die by the blade.

58. MAINE IS THE ONLY STATE IN THE CONTINENTAL UNITED STATES THAT BORDERS ONLY ONE OTHER STATE.

Go check on a map.

59. IN TENNESSEE, IT'S ILLEGAL TO USE A LASSO TO CATCH A FISH.

· 60 ·

ANTARCTICA IS A DESERT.

There are large portions of land where it's believed that no rain has fallen for over two million years! Lack of rainfall and aridity are what define a desert, not sand.

• 61 •

TRUE OR FALSE? THE HUMAN NOSE IS ABLE TO DETECT MORE THAN ONE BILLION SMELLS.

False. It's more like one trillion! According to a study from 2014, our 400 scent receptors really can detect such an incredible amount. Who knew there were so many?

62. TRUE OR FALSE? MINNESOTA HAS MORE SHORELINE IN TOTAL THAN CALIFORNIA, FLORIDA, AND HAWAII COMBINED.

True. But only if you include its rivers and streams. Still, even without those, it has more shoreline than California and Hawaii combined. It's all the lakes. So many lakes.

63. TRUE OR FALSE? THE EMPIRE STATE BUILDING HAS ITS OWN ZIP CODE.

True. It's 10118, in case you need to send something there.

64. TRUE OR FALSE? BUBBLE WRAP WAS ORIGINALLY SUPPOSED TO BE USED AS WALLPAPER.

True. It was created by putting two shower curtains together, which created bubbles between them. The idea didn't catch on, but it made a splendid packing product.

65. TRUE OR FALSE? THE EIFFEL TOWER WAS ORIGINALLY MEANT FOR LONDON.

False. It was meant for Barcelona, but they didn't want it. Their loss.

66. TRUE OR FALSE? COWS HAVE REGIONAL ACCENTS.

True. A study of West Country cows in England determined that cows from different areas had slightly different moos.

67. TRUE OR FALSE? RENO, NEVADA, IS FARTHER WEST THAN LOS ANGELES.

True. Check it on a map.

68. TRUE OR FALSE? A DENTIST INVENTED COTTON CANDY.

True. Dentist William Morrison and confectioner John C. Wharton invented it in 1897, and it really caught on a few years later. Morrison probably just wanted to make sure he had a steady stream of new patients.

• 69 •

TRUE OR FALSE? UNTIL 1915, ONE COULD LEGALLY MAIL A BABY IN THE UNITED STATES.

True. Children had stamps attached to their clothing and traveled on a train, but they were technically "mailed." It was made a federal crime in 1920.

70. TRUE OR FALSE? FEBRUARY 1865 IS THE ONLY MONTH IN RECORDED HISTORY NOT TO HAVE A FULL MOON.

False. Februaries without full moons aren't that unusual. It's an interval called the Metonic cycle, and happens every nineteen years, most recently in 2018.

71. TRUE OR FALSE? THE LOUVRE IN PARIS IS SO LARGE THAT IT WOULD TAKE A HUNDRED DAYS TO VIEW EACH PIECE.

True, sort of. Only a fraction of its collection is viewable at any given time, about 35,000 pieces. If you only viewed those for thirty seconds at a time, it would still take more than twelve days to see them all.

72. TRUE OR FALSE? PLAY-DOH WAS ORIGINALLY MEANT TO PATCH UP HOLES IN WALLS.

False. It was invented to be a wallpaper cleaner.

73. TRUE OR FALSE? INDIA HAS A BILL OF RIGHTS FOR COWS.

False. Not a Bill of Rights per se, but the Indian constitution does uphold the legality of laws prohibiting the slaughter of cows for religious reasons.

74. TRUE OR FALSE? KLEENEX TISSUES WERE FIRST USED AS FILTERS IN GAS MASKS.

True. They were developed in 1915 to be used during gas attacks in World War I, and they worked pretty well.

• 75 •

TRUE OR FALSE? CATS DELIVERED MAIL IN BELGIUM.

True. In the 1870s, the city of Liège had the bizarre idea of making thirty-seven cats available to carry mail. Messages were tied around their necks in little waterproof bags. One cat got to its destination in under five hours, others took a day or more. Needless to say, the idea didn't take off.

ABOUT
CIDER MILL PRESS
BOOK PUBLISHERS

Good ideas ripen with time. From seed to harvest, Cider Mill Press brings fine reading, information, and entertainment together between the covers of its creatively crafted books. Our Cider Mill bears fruit twice a year, publishing a new crop of titles each spring and fall.

"Where Good Books Are Ready for Press"

Visit us on the w
cidermillpress.com
or write to us at
PO Box 454
12 Spring St.
Kennebunkport, Maine 04046